AN ANTHOLOGY OF CATHOLIC POETS

A

AN ANTHOLOGY OF
CATHOLIC POETS

Compiled by

SHANE LESLIE

NEW YORK
THE MACMILLAN COMPANY
1926

ACKNOWLEDGEMENTS

The thanks of the Editor are due to the
following publishers for permission to
include poems issued by them in the
American edition of this book : To Messrs.
Dodd, Mead and Co. for three poems by
Ernest Dowson and one by Aubrey
Beardsley, and to Messrs. G. P. Putnam's
Sons, Ltd., for three poems by Oscar Wilde.

PRINTED IN THE UNITED STATES OF AMERICA BY
THE BERWICK & SMITH CO.

CONTENTS

v

CONTENTS

CONTENTS

CONTENTS

THE MARTYRS

ELIZABETHANS

CONTENTS

CONTENTS

CONTENTS

THE HOLY WOMEN

xi

CONTENTS

THE IRISH

xii

CONTENTS

THE LITERARY MOVEMENT

CONTENTS

THE LITERARY MOVEMENT

THIS WREATH, GATHERED FROM DEAD POETS, PRIESTS, AND LAYMEN, ALL OF WHOM, AND SOME WITH THEIR BLOOD ACKNOWLEDGED THE HOLY SEE, IS OFFERED AT THE THRONE-STEPS OF THE ROMAN PONTIFF, NOW GLORIOUSLY REGNANT OVER URB AND ORB

AN ANTHOLOGY OF CATHOLIC POETS

INTRODUCTION

THIS is a Catholic Anthology, but within certain limits of a term, which might mean embracing different lands and languages. Vague and vagabond Anthologies are an oppression to the modern shelf. This collection wanders through a thousand years of English letters, but it returns to the meridian of Rome. The English authors selected all died in communion with the Holy See. From Anglo-Saxon beginnings Rome fed and fostered England, and England became England under a Roman aura. Until the sixteenth century every English poet was Catholic, so that the great burst of anonymous lyrics and ballads may be accounted a Catholic growth. After the Reformation Catholic poets became stray singers amongst a remnant like Habington or Davenant, converts to an unpopular minority like Dryden, rarities or prodigies like Pope, and sometimes stars rising to martyrdom like Southwell.

This book only indicates the lines of such an Anthology, for separate collections could be made from the medieval writers or from the classical temples of Dryden and Pope, or from the modern heralds and aftermath of the Oxford Movement. While genuine flowers of poetry from the meads of asphodel are not lacking, some pieces have been included as specimens for a hieratic herbarium. Others are included for their writers' sake or for their allusion to Catholic tenets

1

or history. In an arbitrary way some are excluded who wrote beautiful poetry but lost the Faith, like John Donne, who, though of the blood of the Blessed Thomas More, preferred to be a Dean of St Paul's instead of joining Crashaw as a Canon of Loretto. Marvell, *mirabile dictu*, became a Catholic, but relapsed. Wycherley was converted and reconverted, but returned in his last moments. Montague Summers, his learned editor, writes: " There can be no doubt at all that he died a Catholic. All that business with Dr. Barlow at Oxford was just fudge. Wycherley should certainly be included in a book of poems by Catholic writers." Ben Jonson slipped in and out of the Church, thereby becoming too rare even for this collection. The sublime sonnet on Night by Blanco White is omitted because the author-priest benighted himself in the end. Rossetti, on his death-bed, asked his friends in vain for a priest, though who shall say he failed to enter into the House of Life ? In virtue of final submission we include the work of men like Hawker of Morwenstow and Oscar Wilde, who became Catholics in their last hours, though Father Matthew Russell believed that the author of *De Profundis*, which is a Catholic prose-poem, had been privately baptised in a Catholic Church in Dublin as a child. Aubrey Beardsley and W. H. Mallock were also converts before death.

The poems are not necessarily religious. The ethical, the amatory, the epigrammatic and the political have been strung to the gamut. The controversial has been avoided, though one Hymn of Hate has been included from the ballads of Penal times, which, though a derisive dirge over the failure of the Catholic Rising in the North, echoes in pathetic refrain the name of a martyred priest. Balladry, which had grown flowerlike from Catholic soil, withered with the Reformation

2

INTRODUCTION

The Protestant Broadside proved only a nettle growing among the ruins of that past which is fitly mourned in the *Wreck of Walsingham*.

A Catholic Anthology may well commence with a paraphrase of that magnificent *Dream of the Rood* which survives in part on the Ruthwell Cross. Out of the Anglo-Saxon murk glows that ghostly gallows-tree, made beautiful in some unknown poet's vision unto gold and gore. There is an unearthly gleam in the death of St Guthlac, whose soul quits a trembling England, and amid the play of Northern lights enters a Heaven of " winsome wold," but early English poetry is no match for the Irish. Beowulf is small beer compared to the rich honey ale of the Cuchulain Saga. England produced no bardic system, so conscientious monks did their best with poems like *Ormulum* in twenty thousand lines, which is naturally difficult to anthologise, or the longer and even more popular piece of universal history called *Cursor Mundi*. The Benedictine John Lydgate, irreproachable in ritual or rhythm, wrote reams of pious matter, from which it is curious to see him turn to write a Mass to Venus. But the Medievals believed so fast and firm that they can afford to frighten timid souls sometimes. In Lydgate's train comes Alexander Barclay, whose *Ship of Fools* was the most read didactic poem of the time. It is chiefly translated matter, but quite uninspired, a graft of Tupper's *Proverbial Philosophy* on the scholastic sap. Novels and newspapers were lacking, and the literate devoted a corresponding attention to their Bibles. The advent of the Flood or the adventures of Jonah were accorded the literary honours of the best modern fiction. A far-away lyric recalls days when Ely was still an island, inhabited by the monks whose chant could be heard by a Danish King rowing across

3

the fens. With the coming of Norman Kings, French and Latin became the literary tongues, but in Legendaries of still Saxon speech the great Anglo-Norman saints and heroes loomed like the figures in a stained window. Thomas, the blissful martyr of Canterbury, obsessed the hero-worshipping mind of England as deeply as General Gordon, and became as popular pictorially as Mr. Chaplin.

In the great jungle of medieval epic and ballad, the Antiquary must go hand in hand with the Anthologist. All the Arthurian legend is a wild flower growing out of the gargoyles of the Sanctuary. With what a perfect oxymoron King Arthur makes his Confession—" with lamentable cheer." There was a Catholic vocabulary growing like a core within English. The Medievals had special words for certain great relics in Rome. The *Vernicle* was St Veronica's napkin, and the *Palmalle* was the stone of *Domine, quo vadis?* imprinted by the Divine Face and Foot respectively. Religion gave English scores of phrases and words now lost or misunderstood, culminating in the splendid line in which Shakespeare (who knew the Old Religion, as possibly the Old Religion knew him) expressed three Sacraments in three words:

" unhouseled, unappointed, unanealed."

English was planted afresh in great glory by William Langland and Geoffrey Chaucer. Chaucer displays every type possible among the medieval bourgeoisy as they took road to Canterbury. Such a national galaxy could only be found to-day on the way to the Derby. Langland envisioned the mystic ploughman, the swinking toiler with his bitter wrongs who is transfigured in the dyed garments of Christ. Against this sublimity set the amazing ale-house scene which makes the native setting for the Deadly Sin of Gluttony. Lang-

4

land's language is strong and primitive; quaint too, when we read of " the *all-witty* Father " (all-knowing) and Mary " the *clean* mother " (pure), as our forefathers called them. Satire of the unworthy clergy rises fiercely in both writers, as it always has in countries where the Faith is strong and the laity cherish a high clerical standard. Satire of the clergy ceases not from Chaucer's Friars to Skelton's sporting parson, with whom we somewhat sympathise, although—

> On Saint John's Decollation
> He hawked on this fashion
> *Tempore Vesperarum*
> *Sed non secundum Sarum !*

Chaucer one day retracted with sorrow his " enditings of worldly vanities," by which he meant his inclusion of Boccacian novelettes amid such exquisite Catholic idylls as the Second Nun's Tale of St Cecily or the Prioress' Tale of the little schoolboy done to death by Jews. It is impossible to believe that Jews ever committed such ghastly crimes, but the medieval imagination symbolised " the Jewish peril " in such recurring guise. From a literary point of view Chaucer and Shakespeare were terrible anti-Semites. It was quite possible neither had ever seen a Jew even in Gabardine. Chaucer's poor Parson remains the medieval Father O'Flynn, and his blusterous Shipman prefigured the Nelsonic creations of Dibdin and Marryat. Certain it is that all types of the old Faith ride upon Chaucer's Canterbury road, and that Chaucerian English florifies like a garden of wild and foreign plants, domestic and exotic mixed. Take only the catalogue of Alchemy, which with her no less sinister sister Astrology played so great a part in the Catholic curiosity of the Middle Ages. What wealth of words !

Descensories,
Vials, croslets and sublimatories,
Cucurbites and alembics eke:
Rubyfying waters and bull's gall,
Arsenic, sel of ammonia and brimstone
And herbs could I tell many one eke
As agrimony, valerian and lunary.
Our furnace too of calcination
And of water's albification.

If Shakespeare was to become high noon, Chaucer was the mellow sunrise of English letters. Poets' Corner in Westminster Abbey grew round his ashes. It is curious that his descendants the De La Poles came near to the Throne, and that there was a connection between the author of the *Canterbury Tales* and the last Catholic Archbishop buried in the Cathedral. But the old Catholic England, that was so intense and so insular, innocent and insolent, perished, and nothing remains except the cathedral super-shrines and a mass of manuscript literature, the prey of Anglicans and antiquaries respectively.

The whole Elizabethan flower burst from the old literary stalk that Catholic scribes and poets had built blindly and coralwise through the centuries. The English lyric had been trained upon the rigid, exquisite rhyming Latin hymns, and the English Drama had beginnings in the famous Miracle Plays like English hops blossoming from their nursing poles. Minstrels, Franciscans and Troubadours were each others' counterpart. Half the love poetry of England was channelled into service of our Lady, whom her singers hailed as the sweetest of " Mays," just as they did not fear to call our Lord the " leman " of the soul. It is difficult to realise the Marial power in the Middle Ages. England alone was her Dowry from Walsingham to Wales. She was the Janitress of Heaven, the Portress of Purgatory, and even " the Empress of Hell."

6

To Limbo sent our Lady, our Lord, and the great power and part of Mary in the Redemption was excused in the perennial palindrome of " Eva " and " Ave." Perhaps there was more love in medieval religion than fear, for of many love lyrics the religious parody is often recognisable. Men likewise expressed their deepest feeling, even of love or hate, in the familiar phrases of Holy Church. Hence the bitter parodies of Latin hymns which greeted the death of the royal minion Piers Gaveston :

Pange lingua necem Petri qui turbavit Angliam

But this poem and the grim imitation of the *Vexilla Regis* used on the same occasion belong to an overdue Anthology of the Latin Verse which has been written in England during the last thousand years. The Catholic touch was not absent even from drinking songs, as the jolly refrain reminds us to—

> Bring us in good ale and bring us in good ale:
> For Our Blessed Lady's sake bring us in good ale.

But the national drink did not pass wholly without reproach in Merry England :

> Ale makes many a man to swear by God and All Hallows,
> And ale makes many a man to hang upon the gallows.

Both Catholic and Protestant writers (Langland and Latimer) complained that rhymes of Robin Hood were popularly preferred to Paternoster or preaching. But howsoever little Robin loved Abbots and Bishops, he heard three Masses every day before he dined, and—

> Robin loved Our dear Lady;
> For doubt[1] of deadly sin
> Would he never do company harm
> That any woman was in.

---

[1] Fear.

Robin Hood and King Arthur were as much of the Old Religion as the Fairies and the Friars who once haunted English lanes and hills.

Wars against the foreign Fleur-de-lys abroad or for rural Roses at home added little to English poetry. There was Laurence Minot, a Plantagenet Kipling, who dealt with Scots and Frenchmen as lesser breeds without the Law; and Skelton, who, however much he hated heretics and Cardinal Wolsey, loved the birds. His praise of a living parrot and a dead sparrow is part of the Aviary of Song to which Gerard Hopkins was to contribute the mystical Windhover he dedicated " to Christ our Lord."

With Tudorism the stream of national life divides. " England's merriest Chancellor is dead," and the Avon hears the swan-song of the old religion. Books are still written to prove the Catholicism or Protestantism of Shakespeare. He was a Janus looking both ways, but, like many an English mind, acquaint with the Catholic order, he found its only substitute in a gracious scepticism, the religion of all wise men who have not seen the Star. Of the Elizabethan dramatic Pleiad, only Massinger and Shirley can be reckoned Catholics. But Lodge and Byrd and Constable were marvellous strong song-sters beating against cloud. John Heywood, whom Lamb styled a " prose Shakespeare," may be claimed Catholic for the allegory rather than the inspiration of his Protestant Spider and Catholic Fly. Catholic verse soon became the occasional cry of a persecuted minority torn between their religious and their temporal allegiances under Elizabeth and James, martyred for Charles the First and exiled with James the Second. The martyrs write from the Tower. More and Southwell were the flower of the sacrifice made in English Prose and Poetry to the old Catholic order. Southwell's grandmother was a Shelley, and to have written his *Burning · Babe*, Ben Jonson said that he would have ignited some of his own bantlings. Certain it is that Shakespeare read Southwell, a favourite poet during England's golden age, and Southwell doubtless alludes to Shakespeare's *Venus and Adonis* in the pathetic lines:

> This makes my mourning Muse resolve in tears,
> This themes my heavy pen to plain in prose,
> Christ's thorn is sharp, no head His garland wears,
> Still finest wits are 'stilling Venus' rose.

Saint Peter's Complaint was Southwell's pathetic attempt to make the sacred Muse dance as prettily as the profane. The stanzas read like gashes rather than gushes of song. Never was the antithesis between Love and Lust more sincerely sung than by Southwell, whose body was constantly tortured in the Tower betwixt the ecstasies of his soul. The sad little antiphrases permeating his unsmiling song almost seem studied upon the rack.

Henry Walpole and Chidiock Tichborne represent those old families who would not renegate from the Faith, but there were a thousand more who do not come within poetry's net. Their lot is well described in Dryden's satire on the Popish Plot.

Catholic royalism was lit by the seraphic Crashaw, and the Restoration is marked by the rakish Wycherley. Cowley imaged Crashaw as himself carried, like the Virgin's House, by angels to Loretto:

> 'Tis surer much they brought thee there, and they
> And thou their charge went singing all the way.

Crashaw touched Catholic imagery at its best and its worst. His image of St Teresa was chryselephantine in its beauty of ivory and gold. But his weeping Magdalen was worse than

9

·maudlin. Only a modern plaster statue could exhibit
eyes like

> Two faithful fountains;
> Two walking baths, two weeping motions,
> Portable and compendious fountains !

Sir William Davenant, the godson of Shakespeare and friend
of Milton, was the convert laureate who succeeded the
apostate Ben Jonson; and if Protestants can claim the glorious
Revolution, Catholics claim the glorious John Dryden, who,
it is interesting to note, spells Achitophel in his greatest satire
according to the Douay Version. With the Revolution,
Dryden was ousted by the very Shadwell whom he had derided
as " the last great prophet of tautology." It was a Catholic
priest, Flecknoe, who lent his name to the satire of both
Dryden and Pope on the dullard and the dunce. Dryden was
a convert and the laureate of the Jacobites, singing the birth
of the Old Pretender or the death of Dundee. In words of
beaten brass he satirised the Popish Plot and its plotter Titus
Oates as " Coran " :

> His long chin proved his wit, his saint-like grace
> A Church vermilion,[1] and a Moses' face.
> His memory, miraculously great,
> Could plots exceeding Man's belief relate.

Dryden made Rhyme and Reason one. It is curious that
both he and Pope, who each dominated a period, should have
been Catholic. If they did not exhaust the Faith, they
certainly exhausted the Catholic Muse. Pope's verse has been
likened to St Paul's Cathedral, except that it is apparently
more enduring. His verse was dedicated to Pallas rather
than to Apollo. *The Rape of the Lock*, written to close a
quarrel between two Catholic families, was brilliant trifling
reduced to brief baroque, but *The Essay on Man* might well

---

[1] Worm.

be one of the poems which mankind will carry into another civilisation. The gap in Catholic letters remained unfilled even by the trickle supplied by the amusing and reverend Francis Mahony and Alexander Geddes.

After Pope, Catholic letters suffered a total lapse. Before the nineteenth century dawned, the " Papist," the English Recusant, should have become extinct as a type. The Catholic Englishman whose traditions were based on Glastonbury and Canterbury, and later on Douay and Downside, Stonyhurst and Rheims, seemed a sullen alien or an ecstatic exotic—a traitor to England's Protestant soul. He might easily have died out with badger-baiting and the House of Stuart. But with the clarion of the Oxford Movement the tides were turned in their courses. Under the influence of Scott, Young England idealised the literary forms of the Old Faith. Rome and Romance seemed one, and both Poesy and Cleresy in England peeped Popeward. Upon the rolling wave of ten thousand converts, the voice of the poet was audible—Newman, Faber, and Coventry Patmore, whom Mrs. Meynell placed " 'twixt Anacreon and Plato." In Faber, London received an apostle if England, as Wordsworth said, lost a poet. In Newman, Oxford lost an apostle and Birmingham acquired a poet. In one pathetic poem, mistaken by all the Churches for a hymn, Newman united English-speaking Christians. In the great operatic piece of *Gerontius* he fascinated Englishmen to vision into the Catholic afterworld. It was an Apologia for Catholicism, not for Newmanism. In Coventry Patmore, Anglican Deaneries lost the Angel of their House, who, after conversion, was rapt into the secrets of the Seventh Sphere, *non Anglicanus sed Angelus*. The change from *The Angel in the House* to the *Divine Eros* is the most salient in the history of poetry. From sublimated domesticity the reader is translated to the passions of the seraphic soul. Equally he sang Mary and Marriage, amorist of both. Patmore placed Marriage (in entire antithesis to Meredith's *Modern Love*) upon the pinnacle of the romantic. To him Marriage was not the dull drug that lovers are sugar-snared into swallowing like children in some old-fashioned apothecary's, but the apotheosis of Love itself. Even for a Victorian writer it was paradoxical, but the impulse proved divine, and it carried the poet from Sarum Close to the side of St John of the Cross.

Great poetical possibilities were lost in Gerard Hopkins and in Hawker of Morwenstow. Hopkins became a Jesuit in Ireland, and Hawker remained a Cornish parson, to come into the Church on his death-bed, bearing a few fragments, which showed he had the faith and fire which Tennyson lacked in his otherwise peerless dealing with the Holy Graal. Reminiscently of Crashaw's most famous Latin line, Hawker wrote hauntingly of Transubstantiation:

> The vessel of the Pasch, Shere-Thursday[1] night,
> The self-same cup wherein the faithful wine
> Heard God, and was obedient unto blood !

Gerard Hopkins' poems remained hidden like violets, while his whole life became a passion-flower in the Jesuit Conservatory, like some lesser light in that Trinity, which with Patmore and Francis Thompson marks a corona rather than a corner in the poetic sky. Patmore called the poems of Hopkins "pure gold in unpracticable quartz." To Thompson, Patmore was "the greatest genius of the century," while to Patmore, Thompson's *Hound of Heaven* was "one of the few great odes that the language can boast." Within a short period of years Patmore and Thompson brought English

[1] **Maundy** Thursday.

religious poetry to unsuspected, perhaps unsurpassable, heights. Even the fiery Spaniards St Teresa, Raymond Lull and St John of the Cross (sanctity apart) did not reach much further than these choice poets of Anglican descent. Patmore sang of soaring erotically unto the Beloved and Divine, and Thompson of the flight of the timid soul from an all-searching, all-consuming Lover. For them the broad-pinioned Ode, but Hopkins only essayed broken metres and disappearing sevenths to express the thoughts of an ascetic too reserved in his inner life to burst into flame. Technically he seems a casualty to his own cadences. He arranged his words sometimes like coloured counters of mosaic and some-times like the notes in a harmony of music. His poems are handed down by the initiated not like candles of flame or glowing coals, but like enamels that have run into each other with intensity of heat upon a reliquary. He has remained hidden except for the little-known collections revealed by Canon Beeching and Robert Bridges. It has been supposed that the Poet Laureate kept back some poems of an over-enthusiastic character to the Virgin. Mr. Bridges has kindly written to say: " I was guided entirely by what I knew his prayers and wishes had been. The only poem that I was really sorry to suppress was the long school poem *A Vision of Mermaids*, which is a remarkable performance." It is unlikely, then, that any more are likely to appear, for the poet practised with himself the same literary holocaust which he innocently caused to a work of Patmore. Close to the names of Patmore and Thompson must come the name of Alice Meynell, in whose tomb the Catholic Muse must sleep awhile. She was the link between them. To her Thompson wrote the poems of which Patmore said that Laura would have been proud.

Conjointly with the Oxford Movement came the Irish

Diaspora. The famished forties brought restlessness to Irish labour as well as to Oxford intellect. Irish laity, Irish priests, Irish churches filled Celtic ghettos in the great English towns. England had compelled her language upon Ireland, and Ireland responded with a galaxy of Anglo-Irish poetry to express her own embittered memories and faith. A Catholic Anthology cannot be wholly English or Irish, for the charity of the Church covers a multitude of patriotisms. Patriotism is not among the Beatitudes or canonical virtues. Irish patriotism has been made over-synonymous with Catholicism, and there is no truer patriot than the English Catholic, who, because he has given the Pope complete spiritual allegiance, remains more loyal than the King. The Irish echo in poetry can be traced from Moore and Mangan to the Fenian and Sinn-Fein singers. Among them John Boyle O'Reilly was the only convict to appear in *The Oxford Book of English Verse*. There need be no apology for men whom Englishmen have forgiven for dying for their country, though it was not England, for there were Irishmen who pathetically died for England believing it was for Ireland.

The compiler's apologies are due to many poets whose rights to copy or curtail do not exist. Not only have many poems been relentlessly clipped, but spelling has often been modernised and synonyms interchanged. In Medieval English there was one beautiful handwriting but many spellings, to which succeeded standard spelling and many not lovely hands. The great bulk of Middle English escapes the modern reader's eye chiefly on account of unfamiliar spelling, but it does seem unnecessary to the sense to write Syria " Surrey," or trifles " trufles," or fleur-de-lys " flour-de-lice." If new readers are lured to the unknown author

of *Sir Gawain and the Green Knight*, to Langland and
Chaucer, this method will not have been in vain. A fair
number of the old words have been retained with glosses
at the foot ; words that often deserve to live and reward
the reader for their beauty or felicity. The essence of
Anthologies is personal. It is the literary equivalent to the
Japanese art of arranging flowers. The Anthologist must
choose to please himself alone. For that reason this is not an
exhibition of the best specimens of the best authors. Where
the compiler has been interested in a poet like Habington,
Constable or Gerard Hopkins, he has plucked lavishly
and dwelt lingeringly. Chaucer and Pope should from a
literary value have possessed half the volume, for each made an
era, and significantly their names are the only Catholic names
written in gold under the dome of the Reading Room in the
British Museum. They were great moulders of the English
language who happened to be Catholics. Coventry Patmore
and Francis Thompson wrote because they were Catholic,
and Catholic poetry flows to their high-water mark and thence
recedes. In an age of multiplying books and dwindling style,
of formlessness and insipidity of taste and mushiness of matter,
the compiler implores equally readers, who would become
good writers; and writers, who would become good readers,
to make unto themselves a chrestomathy of Geoffrey Chaucer
and Alexander Pope.

Finally, from the Literary Movement come the penitential
verses of Oscar Wilde, Wilfrid Blunt, Ernest Dowson, and
Lionel Johnson, relieved by a light phantasy of Aubrey
Beardsley, for it is a long lane which does not lead to
Rome.

The compiler's thanks are due to volumes distinguished
by the fine editorship of Sir Israel Gollancz, Skeat, Chambers

and Sidgwick, A. H. Bullen, the Early English Text Society, the Percy and Ballantyne and Roxburgh publications.

Also to Mr. Robin Flower, of the British Museum, who called attention to the Add. MS. 15225, which is a collection of Catholic verse of Penal times. The only other poems taken from manuscript are Constable's sonnet to St Mary Magdalen, which is copied from Harleian MS. 7553, and Southwell's "Execution of Mary, Queen of Scots," which appears as "*Morior Orior*" in Add. MS. 10422.

Also to Miss Anne Brindley for her unwearied assistance in the Libraries of the British Museum and Greatham; to Miss Joyce Lowe, who kindly contributed her unpublished collection; to Mr. Wilfrid Meynell, who lent his fine taste and knowledge in all Catholic Poetry as well as the encouragement to complete this book.

Also for use of copyright in the following cases: For poems by Oscar Wilde to Messrs. Methuen; for poems by Tom Kettle to Mrs. Kettle; for a poem by Francis Ledwidge to Lord Dunsany; for poems by Ernest Dowson and a poem by Aubrey Beardsley to John Lane, Ltd.; for a poem by Joseph Plunkett to Mrs. Joseph Plunkett; for poems by Lionel Johnson to Elkin Mathews, Ltd.; for poems by Francis Thompson and poems by Alice Meynell to Mr. Wilfrid Meynell; for poems by Fr. Gerard Hopkins to Mr. Gerard Hopkins; for poems by W. H. Mallock to Miss Mallock; for a poem by Dora Sigerson to Mr. Clement Shorter; for a poem from the Collected Poems of Thomas Macdonagh to the Talbot Press of Dublin.

May their souls and the souls of all dead makars repose in eternal lucency. ✠

ANGLO-SAXON

CAEDMON

(SEVENTH CENTURY)

The Approach of Pharaoh

. . . THEN they saw
Forth and forward faring, Pharaoh's war array,
Gliding on, a grove of spears; glittering the hosts !
Fluttered there the banners, there the folk the march trod.
Onwards surged the war, strode the spears along,
Blickered the broad shields; blew aloud the trumpets.
Wheeling round in gyres, yelled the fowls of war,
Of the battle greedy; hoarsely barked the raven,
Dew upon his feathers, o'er the fallen corpses;
Swart that chooser of the slain !   Sang aloud the wolves
At the eve their horrid song, hoping for the carrion
Kindless were the beasts, cruelly they threaten;
Death did these march-warders, all the midnight through,
Howl along the hostile trail—hideous slaughter of the host

(Translated from " Genesis.")

CYNEWULF

(EIGHTH CENTURY)

Death of Saint Guthlac

. . . THEN out-streamed a Light
Brightest that of beaming pillars ! All that Beacon fair,
All that heavenly glow round the holy home,
Was upreared on high, even to the roof of Heaven,
From the field of earth, like a fiery tower,
Seen beneath the sky's expanse, sheenier than the sun,
Glory of the glorious stars ! Hosts of angels sang
Loud the lay of Victory ! In the lift the ringing sound
Now was heard the heaven under, raptures of the Holy Ones !
So the blessed Burgstead was with blisses filled,
With the sweetest scents, and with skiey wonders,
With the angels' singing, to its innermost recesses;
   Heirship of the Holy One !
                     More onelike it was,
And more winsome there, than in world of ours
Any speech may say; how the sound and odour,
How the clang celestial, and the saintly song
Heard in Heaven were—high-triumphant praise of God,
Rapture following rapture.
                  All our island trembled,
All its Field-floor shook.

(Translated from " Guthlac.")

ANONYMOUS

(EIGHTH CENTURY)

The Dream of the Rood

The Holy Cross speaks:

I AM remembering in the long ago:
   How at the forest-edge they hewed me low,
And stem-cut thence strong foes took me to stare
Upon and bade me outcast men to bear
And hillward bore me shoulder high and then
Foes fixed me there.   I saw the Lord of men
In his might hastening there me to ascend,
Yet dared not break asunder nor me bend
Nor disobey for God's commandment's sake
Though Earth I saw in all her bosom quake.
I stood, who might have thrown the foes to sod.
Then gathered Him, the Warrior young called God
Almighty; resolute and strong; unbowed
Of courage went He up in sight of crowd
Upon the lofty Cross mankind to fend.
I trembled in His arms but dared not bend
Or earthward fall: but firmly had to stand.
On me, the Cross, the mighty King was spanned
The Heaven's Lord, yet dared I not to quail.
You see the Wounds, dark piercing of the Nail
And open gashes.   To none dared bring I bane.
They scorned us both and I was made astain
With Blood forth from His Side that flowed,
When He like Man His Ghost sent on its road.
And many were the bitter pangs I bore
Upon that hill.   The Lord of Hosts I saw

ANONYMOUS

Unkindly set upon and darkness shroud
The Ruler's corpse with covering of cloud.
In face of shadowy night day's splendour leapt
All wan beneath the welkin. All creation wept.

The Grave

FOR thee a stead was builded
 Ere thou wast born,
For thee was mould shapen
Ere thou of mother came.
The heel-ways are low,
Side-ways unhigh.
The roof is builded
Thy breast full nigh:
So thou shalt in mould
Dwell full cold,
Dim and dark.
Doorless is that house
And dark it is within;
There thou beest fast betied
And Death holdeth the key.
Loathly is that earth-house
And grim within to dwell ;
There thou shalt dwell
And worms thee divide.
Thus thou beest laid
And leavest thine friends,
Thou hast none friend
That thee will fare unto
That ever will look in
How that house thee liketh,
That ever will undo
For thee the door
And thee after hasten,
For soon thou beest loathly
And laid to see upon.

THE MEDIEVAL

ROBERT MANNING OF BRUNNE

(1288–1338)

The Round Table

FOR no man wist who was best
Nor in arms doughtiest—
Did he ordain the Round Table
That men tell of many fable.
None sat within, none sat without,
But all ever round about;
None sat first, none sat last,
But peer by peer ever cast;
None sat high, none sat low,
But all evenly for to know;
None was set at the end,
But all around and all were hende;[1]
None wist who of them most was,
For they sat all in compass;
All at once, down they sitten,
At once rose, when they had eaten,
All were served of a service,
Evenly all of an assize

[1] Gentle.

The Bishop's Harp

NEXT his chamber, beside his study
  His harper's chamber was fast the by.
Many times, by nights and days,
He had solace of notes and lays.
One asked him the reason why
He had delight in minstrelsy:
He answered him in this manner
Why he held the harp so dear:
The virtue of the harp through skill and right
Will destroy the fiend's might;
And to the cross by good skill
Is the harp likened well.

RICHARD ROLLE, Hermit

(1290–1349)

Love is Life

FOR now, love thou, I rede, Christ, as I thee tell:
   And with Angels take thy stead; that joy look thou
norght sell!
In earth thou hate, I rede, all that thy love may fell:
For Love is stalworth as the death, Love is hard as hell.

Love is a light burden, Love gladdeth young and old;
Love is without pine, as lovers have me told;
Love is a ghostly wine, that makes men big and bold:
Of Love shall he nothing tyne[1] that it in heart will hold.

But fleshly love shall fare as doth the flower in May
And lasting be no more than one hour of a day,
And sithen sigh full sore their lust, their pride, their play,
When they are cast in care, till pine that lasteth aye.

Jesu is Love that lasteth aye: to Him is our longing:
Jesu the night turneth to day, the dawning into spring.
Jesu think on us now and aye: for Thee we hold our King;
Jesu give us grace, as Thou well may, to love Thee withoui
   ending.

(From "Love is Life.")

[1] Lose.

JOHN GOWER

(1325-1408)

Jason and Medea

APPOINTED in the newe Moon,
  When it was time for to done,
She set a caldron on the fire
In which was all the whole attire
Wheron the medecine stood
Of juice, of water and of blood,
And let it boil in such a plight
Till that she saw the spume white,
And though she cast in rind and root,
And seed and flower that was for boot,
With many an herb and many a stone,
Whereof she hath there many one:
And eke Cimpheius the Serpent
To her hath all his scales lent,
Chelidre her gave his adder's skin
And she to boiling cast them in;
A part eke of the horned Owl
The which men hear on nightes howl,
And of a Raven, which was told
Of nine hundred winter old,
She took the head with all the bill;
And as the medecine it will,
She took therefore the bowel
Of the Seawolf and for the heal
Of Jason with a thousand mo
Of thinges that she hadde tho,
In that caldron together as blithe

She put and took then of Olive
A dry branch them with to stir,
The which anon gave flower and bare
And wax all fresh and green again.

(*From " Confessio Amantis.*")

Hours of the Passion

AT Prime Jesus was y-led
Tofore Sir Pilate
There witnesses false and fele[1]
Belowen Him for hate.
They to-stake His sweet head
With one thornen crown;
To Calvary His cross He bear
Well reulichy[2] out of the town.
On cross y-nailed was Jesus
At Sixten tide
Strong thieves hangen they on
Either half His side.
In His pine His strong thirst
Staunched they with gall
So that God's holy Lamb
Of sin wash us all.
At Nones Jesus Christ
Thane hard death deeled
He cried Eloi to His Father,
The soul He gan upyield.
A Knight with one sharp spear
Stung Him in the right side.
Th' earth shoke, the sun dim become,
In thare tide.
Of the Cross He was do
At Evesong's hour;
The strength left lotede[3] in God
Of our Saviour.

[1] Many.   [2] Ruthfully.   [3] Concealed.

WILLIAM OF SHOREHAM

Such death He under-yede
Of life the medecine,
Alas He was y-laid adown
The crown of bliss in pine.
At Compline it was y-bore
To the burying,
That noble corpse of Jesus Christ,
Hope of lives coming.
Well richly it was anoint,
Fulfilled His holy book;
I bid, Lord, Thy passion
To mine mend look.

(From " Hours of the Passion.")

WILLIAM LANGLAND

(1330–1400)

The Palmer

APPARELLED as a Paynim in pilgrim's wise
He bare a bordon[1] bound with a broad list
Like a withe-wind-weed[2] wounden about.
A bowl and a bag he bare by his side,
A hundred phials on his hat sit,
Signs of Syse and shells of Galicia
And many a Cross on his cloak and Keys of Rome,
And the Vernicle[3] before for men should know
And see by his signs whom he had sought.
This folk frayned[4] him first from whence he come?
" From Sinai," he said, " and from our Lord's Sepulchre;
In Bethlehem, in Babylon, I have been in both;
In Armenia, in Alexandria, and in Damask.
Ye may see by my signs that sit on my cap,
I have sought good Saints for my soul's health,
And walked full wide in wet and in dry."

(From " Piers Plowman.")

[1] Staff.   [2] Bind-weed.   [3] Veronica's kerchief.   [4] Asked.

WILLIAM LANGLAND

The Glutton

NOW beginneth Glutton for to go to shrift,
  And carries him to churchward his culp to show.
Fasting on a Friday forth gan he wend.
By Betun's house the brewster that bade him good morrow,
And the brew-wife him asked whither he would ?
" To Holy Church," quoth he, " for to hear Mass,
And sithen sit and be shriven and sin no more."
" I have good ale, gossip; Glutton, wilt thou essay ?"
" What havest thou ?" quoth he. " Any hot spices ?"
" I have pepper and peonies and a pound of garlic,
A farthing worth of fennel-seed for fasting-days."
Then goeth Glutton in and Great-Oaths after.
Sisse the sempstress sat on the bench,
Watte the warrener and his wife drank,
Tom the tinker and two of his knaves,
Hick the hackneyman and Hugh the needler,
Clarice of Cock's Lane, the clerk of the church,
Sir Pierce of Pridie and Purnel of Flaunders,
An hayward and an heremyte, the hangman of Tyburn,
Darew the Dyker with a dozen hirelots
Of porters and of pickpurses and pylede[1] tooth-drawers,
A rybibour and a ratoner,[2] a raker and his knave,
A reaper and a redingking[3] and Rose the disher,
Godfrey the garlic-monger and Griffyn the Welsher,
And of up-holders[4] an heap early by the morrow
Gave Glutton with glad cheer good ale to hansel.
Clement the cobbler cast off his cloak,
And to the New Fair named it to sell.

1 Bald.   2 Rat-catcher.   3 Rad-knight.   4 Auctioneers.

Hick the hackneyman hit his hood after,
And bade Bette the butcher to be on his side.
There were chapmen y-chose the chaffar[1] to praise;
That he that had the hood should not have the cloak;
The better thing by arbitors should bote the worse.
Two rose rapliche[2] and runned together,
And apprised the pennyworths apart by themselves,
And there were others an heap for other should have the worse.
They could nought by their conscience accord for truth,
Till Robin the reaper arise they besought,
And named him an umpire that no debate were.
Hick the hackneyman had the cloak
In covenant that Clement should the cup fill,
And have the hackneyman's hood and hold him y-served;
And who repented rathest should arise after,
And greet Sir Glutton with a gallon of ale.
There was laughing and lakering[3] and " Let go the cup ! "
Bargains and beverages begin to arise,
And setting so till evensong rang, and was sung awhile,
Till Glutton had gulped a gallon and a gill.

* * * * *

With all the woe of the world his wife and his wench
Bare him to his bed and brought him therein;
And after all this excess he had an accidie,[4]
He slept Saturday and Sunday till sun went to rest.
Then awaked he of his wink and wiped his eyes;
The first word that he spake was " ho halt the bolle ? "[5]
His wife and his inwit[6] edwited him of his sin;
To Repentance " have ruth on me," he said,

---

[1] Ware.   [2] Suddenly.   [3] Sporting.
[4] Lethargy.   [5] Bottle.   [6] Conscience

WILLIAM LANGLAND

" Thou Lord that on loft art and all lives shape !
To thee, God, I Glutton guilty me yield.
Of my trespass with tongue I can naught tell how oft
Swore ' Thy soul and Thy sides ' and ' so help me, God
Almighty !' "

(From " Piers Plowman."

WILLIAM LANGLAND

The Vision of Jesus

THUS I awaked and wrote what I had dreamed
And dight me dearly and dude me to Church
To hear wholly the Mass and be houseled[1] after,
In midst of the Mass tho men geden to offering
I fell eftsoons asleep and suddenly me mette[2]
That Piers the Ploughman was painted all bloody
And came in with a cross before the common people,
And right like in all limbs to our Lord Jesu;
And then called I Conscience to ken me the sooth.
Is this Jesus the jouster, quoth I, that Jews duden to die;
Or is it Piers Ploughman? Who painted him so red?
Quoth Conscience and kneeled then: These aren Christ's
     arms,
His colours and his coat-armour, and he that cometh so
     bloody
It is Christ with His Cross, conqueror of Christdom.

(*From " Piers Plowman."*)

[1] Receive communion.   [2] Dreamed.

WILLIAM LANGLAND

The Palace of Truth

SO shalt thou come to a court as clear as the sun,
  The moat is of Mercy. In midst the manor
All the walling is of Wit for Will should not it win.
The cornels be of Christendom that kind to save,
And buttressed with Believe so or thou worthest not saved
All the houres be heled,[1] halls and chambers
With no lead but with love and with leal speech.
The bars are of buxomness[2] as brethren of one womb,
The Bridge called Bidwell[3] that better might thou speed.
Each pillar is of Penance and prayer to Saint,
The hooks are of almsdeed that the gates hangen on,
Grace is called the gateward a good man for sooth,
His man is called Amend you, many man him knoweth
Tell him this ille token "Truth wot the Sooth,
I am sorry for my sins and so shall I ever
And perform the penance that the priest me hight."
Ride to Amend you, weaken you to his master Grace
To open and undo the high gate of Heaven
That Adam and Eve against us all shut
Per Evam janua coeli cunctis clausa est
Et per Mariam virginem iterum patefacta est.
A full belle lady unlocked her grace;
She hath a key and a clyckett, though the King sleep,
And may lead in whom she loveth as her love liketh.

(From " Piers Plowman.")

---

¹ Covered.   ² Obedience.   ³ Pray well.

GEOFFREY CHAUCER

(1340–1400)

Ballad of Good Counsel

FLEE from the press and dwell with soothfastness;
 Suffice unto thy good though it be small,
For hoard hath hate and climbing ticklishness,
Press hath envy and weal blent[1] overall;
Savour no more than thee bihoven shall;
Work well thyself that other folk canst rede;
And Truthe shall deliver, it is no dread.

Tempest thee[2] not all crooked to redresse
In trust of her that turneth as a ball:
Great reste stands in little business;
And eke be ware to spurn against an awl;
Strive not, as doth the crocke with the wall.
Daunt thyself that dauntest others deed,
And Truthe shall deliver, it is no dread.

That thee is sent receive in buxomness:
The wrestling for this world asketh a fall.
Here is no home, here is but wilderness;
Forth, pilgrim, forth ! Forth, beast, out of thy stall !
Know thy country, look up, thank God of all;
Hold the high way and let thy ghost thee lead
And Truthe shall deliver, it is no dread.

---

[1] Blinded.   [2] Vex thee.

GEOFFREY CHAUCER

Merciless Beauty

YOUR eyen two will slay me suddenly,
  I may the beauty of them not sustain,
So woundeth it throughout my hearte keen.

And but your word will healen hastily
My heartes wound, while that it is green,
Your eyen two will slay me suddenly,
I may the beauty of them not sustain.

Upon my truth I see you faithfully
That ye been of my life and death the Queen;
For with my death the truthe shall be seen.
Your eyen two will slay me suddenly,
I may the beauty of them not sustain,
So woundeth it throughout my hearte keen.

GEOFFREY CHAUCER

The Prioress' Tale

THERE was in Asia, in a great city,
   Amonges Christen folk a Jewery,
Sustained by a lord of that country
For foul usure and lucre of vilany,
Hateful to Christ and to his company;
And through the street men mighte ride or wende,
For it was free and open at either end.

A little school' of Christen folk there stood
Down at the further end, in which there were
Children an heap, y-comen of Christen blood,
That learned in that schoole year by year
Such manner doctrine as men used there,
This is to say, to singen and to read,
As smalle children do in their childhead.

Among these children was a widow's son,
A little clergeon[1] seven years of age,
That day by day to school was his wone[2]
And eke also, whereas he saw th' image
Of Christes mother, had he in usage,
As him was taught, to kneel down and say
His *Ave Marie*, as he goeth by the way.

Thus hath this widow her little son y-taught
Our blisful lady, Christes mother dear,
To worship aye and he forgot it naught,
For sely[3] child would all day soone lere;
But aye, when I remember on this matter,
Saint Nicholas stand ever in my presence,
For he so young to Christ did reverence.

---

[1] Chorister.   [2] Wont.   Wondrous.

This little child, his little book learning,
As he sat in the school at his Primer,
He *Alma Redemptoris* hearde sing,
As children learned their Antiphoner;[1]
And, as he durst, he drew him near and near,
And harkened aye the wordes and the note,
Till he the firste verse could all by rote.

Nought wist he what this Latin was to say,
For he so young and tender was of age;
But on a day his fellow gan he pray
T' expounden him this song in his langage,
Or tell him why this song was in usage;
This prayed he him to construe and declare
Full ofte time upon his kneés bare.

His fellow, which that elder was than he,
Answered him thus: " This song I have heard say,
Was maked of our blisful lady free,
Her to salue[2] and eke her for to pray
To been our help and succour when we die.
I can no more expound in this matter;
I learne song, I can but small grammar."

" And is this song maked in reverence
Of Christes mother ?" said this innocent;
" Now certes, I will do my diligence
To con it all, ere Christemass is went;
Though that I for my primer shall be shent,[3]
And shall be beaten thrice in an hour
I will it con, Our Lady for to honour."

Anthem-book.   [2] Salute.   [3] Spoilt.

43

His fellow taught him homeward privily,
From day to day till he could it by rote,
And then he sang it well and boldly
From word to word, according with the note;
Twyes a day it passed through his throat,
To schoolward and homeward when he went;
On Christes mother set was his intent.

As I have said, throughout the Jewery
This little child, as he came to and fro,
Full merrily then would he sing and cry
O *Alma Redemptoris* evermo.
The sweetness hath his hearte pierced so
Of Christes mother, that, to her to pray
He cannot stint of singing by the way.

Our firste foe, the serpent Satanas,
That hath in Jewes heart his waspes nest,
Up swelled and said, " O Hebraic people, alas !
Is this to you a thing which is honest,
That such a boy shall walken as him lest
In your despite and sing of such sentence,
Which is against your lawes reverence ?"

From thence forth the Jewes have conspired
This innocent out of the world to chase;
An homicide thereto have they hired,
That in an alley had a privy place;
And as the child gan forby for to pace,
This cursed Jew him hente[1] and held him fast,
And cut his throat and in a pit him cast.

[1] Caught.

GEOFFREY CHAUCER

I say that in a wardrobe they him threw
Whereas these Jewes purgen their entrail.
O cursed folk of Herodes all new,
What may your evil intent you avail?
Murder will out, certain, it will not fail,
And namely[1] there th' honour of God shall spread,
The blood out crieth on your cursed deed.

" O Martyr, souded[2] to virginity,
Now mayst thou singen, following ever in one
The whitè lamb celestial," quoth she,
" Of which the great Evangelist Saint John
In Patmos wrote, which saith that they that gone
Before this lamb and sing a song all new,
That never, fleshly, women they not knew."

This poor widow awaiteth all that night
After her little child, but he came nought;
For which, as soon as it was dayes light,
With facè pale of dread and busy thought,
She hath at school and elleswhere him sought,
Till finally she gan so far espy
That he last seen was in the Jewery.

With mother's pity in her breast enclosed
She goeth, as she were half out of her mind,
To every placè where she hath supposed
By likelihood her little child to find;
And ever on Christes mother meek and kind
She cried and at laste thus she wrought,
Among the cursed Jewes she him sought.

1 Especially.   2 Confirmed.

45

She frayneth and she prayeth piteously
To every Jew that dwelt in thilke place,
To tell her, if her child went ought forby.
They said: " Nay," but Jesu of His grace
Gave in her thought, inwith a little space,
That in that place after her son she cried
Where he was casten in a pit beside.

O greate God, that performest Thy laud
By mouth of innocents, lo here Thy might !
This gem of chastity, this emerald,
And eke of Martyrdom the ruby bright,
There he with throat y-carven lay upright,
He *Alma Redemptoris* gan to sing
So loud that all the placè gan to ring.

The Christen folk that through the streete went
In comen, for to wonder upon this thing,
And hastily they for the Provost sent;
He came anon withouten tarrying,
And herieth[1] Christ that is of Heaven King,
And eke his Mother, honour of mankind,
And after that, the Jewes leet[2] he bind.

This child with piteous lamentation
Uptaken was, singing his song alway;
And with honour of great procession
They carrien him unto the next Abbey,
His mother swooning by the bier lay:
Unnethe[3] might the people that was there
This newe Rachel bringe from his bier.

[1] Praiseth.   [2] Bade.   [3] Scarcely.

With torment and with shameful death each one
This Provost doth these Jewes for to sterve[1]
That of this murder wist, and that anon;
He woulde not such cursedness observe.
Evil shall have that evil will deserve.
Therefore with wilde horse he did them draw,
And after that he hung them by the law.

Upon his bier aye lieth this innocent
Before the chief altar, while Masse last,
And after that, the Abbot with his convent
Have sped them for to bury him full fast;
And when they holy water on him cast
Yet spake this child when sprayed was holy wate
And sang—O *Alma Redemptoris Mater !*

This Abbot, which that was an holy man
As monkes been or elles oughten be,
This young child to conjure he began,
And said, " O deare child I halse[2] thee,
In virtue of the Holy Trinity,
Tell me what is thy causè for to sing,
Sith that thy throat is cut to my seeming ?"

" My throat is cut unto my necke bone,"
Said this child, " and as by way of kind,
I should have died, yea, long time agoon,
But Jesu Christ, as ye in bookes find,
Wills that His glory last and be in mind,
And for the worship of His Mother dear,
Yet may I sing ' O *Alma* ' loud and clear."

1 **Die.**   2 **Implore.**

47

This well of mercy, Christes mother sweet,
I loved alway, as after my cunning;
And when that I my lifè should forelet
To me she came and bade me for to sing
This anthem verily in my dying,
As ye have hearde and when that I had sung
Methought, she laid a grain upon my tongue.

Wherefore I sing and sing I must certain
In honour of that blisful maiden free,
Till from my tongue off-taken is the grain;
And afterward thus saide she to me,
" My little child, now will I fetche thee
When that the grain is from thy tongue y-take;
Be not aghast, I will thee not forsake."

This holy monk, this abbot, him mean I,
His tongue out-caught and took away the grain,
And he gave up the ghost full softèly.
And when this Abbot had this wonder seen
His salte teares trickled down as rain,
And gruf[1] he fell all plat upon the ground,
And still he lay as he had been y-bounde.

The convent eke lay on the pavement
Weeping and herien[2] Christes Mother dear,
And after that they rise and forth been went
And took away this Martyr from his bier,
And in a tomb of marblestones clear
Enclosen they his little body sweet;
There he is now, God leave us for to meet.

[1] Grovelling.   [2] Praise.

GEOFFREY CHAUCER

O younge Hugh of Lincoln, slain also
With cursed Jews, as it is notable,
For it is but a little while ago;
Pray eke for us, we sinful folk unstable,
That, of His mercy, God so merciable
On us His greate mercy multiply
For reverence of His Mother Mary.

(From the " Canterbury Tales.")

GEOFFREY CHAUCER

The Poor Parson

A GOOD man was there of religion,
   And was a poor Parson of a town;
But rich he was of holy thought and work;
He was also a learned man, a clerk,
That Christes Gospel truly woulde preach;
His parishens devoutly would he teach.
Benign he was and wonder diligent,
And in adversity full patient;
And such he was y-proved ofte sythes.[1]
Full loath were him to cursen for his tythes,
But rather would he given out of doubt
Unto his poor parishens about
Of his offering, and eke of his substance;
He could in little thing have suffisance.
Wide was his parish, and houses far a-sunder,
But he left not, for rain nor thunder,
In sickness nor in mischief, to visit
The farthest in his parish, much and lyte,[2]
Upon his feet, and in his hand a staff.
This noble ensample to his sheep he gave,
That first he wrought, and afterward he taught.
Out of the gospel he those wordes caught.
And this figure he added eke thereto.
That if gold ruste, what shall iron do ?
He sette not his benefice to hire,
And let his sheep encumbered in the mire,
And ran to London, unto Saint Paul's,
To seeken him a chauntery for souls,

[1] Times.   [2] Rich and poor.

Or with a brotherhood to be withhold;
But dwelt at home, and kepte well his fold,
So that the wolf made it not miscarry;
He was a shepherd and no mercenary.
And though he holy were and virtuous,
He was to sinful man not despitous,
Nor of his speeches dangerous nor digne,[1]
But in his teaching discreet and benign.
To drawen folk to Heaven by fairness
By good ensample was his business:
But it were any person obstinate,
Whatso he were, of high or low estate,
Him would he snubben sharply for the nones:
A better priest, I trow that nowhere none is.
He waited after no pomp and reverence,
Nor made him a spiced conscience.
But Christes lore and his apostles twelve
He taught and first he followed it himself.

(From the Prologue to the " Canterbury Tales.")

[1] Proud.

GEOFFREY CHAUCER

The Shipman

THE Parson him answered, " Bendicite !
What aileth the man so sinfully to swear ?"
Our Host answered, " O Jankin, be ye there ?"
" I smell a Lollard in the wind," quoth he.
" Now good man," quoth our Host, " harken me
Abideth for Godes digne Passion,
For we shall have a Predication;
This Lollard here would preach us somewhat."
" Nay by my father's soul ! That shall he not,"
Said the Shipman: " Here shall he nought preach,
He shall no Gospel glosen here nor teach.
We all 'lieve in the great God," quoth he.
" He would sowen some difficulty
Or springen cockle in our clean corn.
And therefore, Host, I warn thee by-forn
My jolly body shall a tale tell
And I shall clinken you so merry a bell
That I shall waken all this company;
But it shall not be of philosophy,
Nor of physic nor termes quaint of law;
There is but little Latin in my maw."

GEOFFREY CHAUCER

Two Invocations of the Virgin

I

WITHIN the cloister blissful of thy sides
    Took man's shape the Eternal Love and Peace
Who of the trine compass Lord and guide is,
Whom Earth and Sea and Heaven out of release
Aye herien[1] and thou, Virgin, wemless[2]
Bore of thy body and dweltest maiden pure,
The creator of every creature.

               (From the Prologue of " The Second Nun's Tale.")

II

O mother maid, O maiden mother free !
O bush unbrent brenning in Moses' sight
That ravishedst down from the Deity
Through thine humbless the Ghost that in thee lit,
Of whose vertue when He thine hearte lit,
Conceived was the Father's Sapience;
Help me to tell it in my reverence.

               (From the Prologue of " The Prioress's Tale.")

[1] Praise.   Speckless.

ANONYMOUS

(FOURTEENTH CENTURY)

The Temptation of Sir Gawain

BUT when that comely he covered his wits
   Swengeth[1] out of the swevens and swereth[2] with haste,
The lady lovely come laughing sweet
Fell over his fair face and featly him kissed;
He welcomes her worthily with a wale[3] cheer;
He seeth her so glorious and gayly attired,
So faultless of her features and of so fine hues,
Wight[4] welling joy warmed his heart;
With smooth smiling and smolt[5] they smoten into mirth,
That all was bliss and bonchef[6] that broke them between
   and wynn;[7]

> They lanced[8] words good,
> Much weal then was therein
> Great peril between them stood
> If not more of her knight mind.

For that prince of price depressed[9] him so thick,
Nurned[10] him so nigh the thread that need him behoved
Or take there her love or lodly[11] refuse;
He cared for his courtesy lest crathen he were,
And more for his mischief if he should make sin
And be traitor to that tolk[12] that that telde[13] had.
" God shield," quoth the shalk,[14] " that shall not befall."
With love-laughing a lit, he laid him beside
All the speeches of specialty that sprang of her mouth.

1 Starts.	**2** Answers.	**3** Worthy.	**4** Brisk.
5 Mild.	**6** Gaiety.	**7** Bliss.	**8** Uttered
9 Vanquished.	**10** Placed.	**11** Rudely.	**12** Man.
13 House.		**14** Knight.	

Quoth that burd[1] to the burn[2] blame ye deserve,
If ye love not that life that ye lie next,
Before all the wyses[3] in the world, wounded in heart,
But if ye have a leman, a liever, that you like better,
And folden[4] faith to that fre[5] fastened so hard
That you loosen not list and that I leave now
And that ye tell me that, now truly I pray you.
For all the loves upon life, layne[6] not the sooth for guile.

      The knight said by Saint John
      And smoothly could he smile
      In faith I weld[7] right none
      Nor none will weld the while.

" That is a word," quoth that wight, " that worst of all,
But I am swared for sooth, that sore methinks
Kiss me now comely and I shall go hethen.
I may but mourn upon mould as may that much loves,
Sighing she stooped down and seemly him kissed
And sithen she severs him fro and says as she stands,
" Now, dear, at this departing, do me this ease,
Give me somewhat of thy gift, thy glove if it were
That I may mind on the one, my mourning to lessen."

" Now I wis," quoth that wight, " I would I had here
The lievest[8] thing for thy love that I in land weld
For ye have deserved forsooth selely[9] oft
More reward by reason than I reche[10] might
But to deal you for drury[11] that vailed but nicht
It is not your honour to have at this time
A glove for a garison[12] of Gawain's gifts

---

[1] Lady.   [2] Knight.   [3] Folk.   [4] Keep.
[5] Noble.   [6] Hide.   [7] Possess.   [8] Dearest
[9] Wondrously.   [10] Give.   [11] Love token.   [12] Reward

And I am here on errand in earth's uncouth
And have no men with no mails with menskful[1] things
That misliketh me, lady, for love at this time
Each tolk must do as he is taen, tas to no ill nor pine.[2]
   " Nay hende[3] of high honours
   Quoth that lovesome under lyne[4]
   " Though I had nought of yours
   Yet should ye have of mine."

Then taketh she her leave and leaves him there
For more mirth of that man must she not get.
When she was gone, Sir Gawain geareth him soon,
Rises and riches him in array noble,
Lays up the lovelace, the lady him gave
Hid it full holdly,[5] there he it eft found
Sithen chevely[6] to the Chapel choses he the way
Privily approached to a priest and prayed him there
That he would list his life and learn him better
How his soul should be saved when he should see Heaven.
There he shrove him surely and shewed his misdeeds
Of the more and the mynne[7] and mercy beseeches
And of absolution he on the segge[8] calls
And he assoiled him surely and set him so clean
As Doomsday should have been dight on the morn.
With comely carols and all kinds joy
As never he did but that day, to the dark night with bliss.

     (From " Sir Gawain and the Green Knight.")

1 Honourable.	2 Grief.	3 Fair one.	4 Linen.
5 Carefully.	6 Swiftly.	7 Less.	8 Knight.

The Queen of Courtesy

"**B**LISSFUL " quoth I, " may this be true ?
    Displeaseth not if I speak error.
Art thou the Queen of Heaven's blue
That all this world shall do honour ?
We lieven[1] on Mary of whom Grace grew,
That bore a bairn of virgin flower;
The crown from her who might remew
But she her passed in some favour ?
    Now for singleness of her douceur
    We call her Phoenix of Araby
    That freless[2] flew of her fasour[3]
    Like to the Queen of Courtesy."

" Courteous Queen," then said that gay,
Kneeling to ground, enfolden her face,
" Makeless Mother and merriest May,
Blessed beginner of every Grace !"
Then rose she up and did restay,
And spake toward me in that space:
" Sir, many here pourchaseth and fongeth[4] prey,
But supplantereth none within this place.
    That Empress all Heaven hath,
    And Earth and Hell in her baily;
    From heritage yet none will she chase
    For she is Queen of Courtesy.

Of Courtesy, as saith Saint Paul,
All are we members of Jesu Christ;
As head and arm and leg and naul
Serve to his body full true and tryst,

1 Believe.   2 Spotless.   3 Form.   4 Getteth.

ANONYMOUS

Right so is every Christian soul
Belonging limb to the Master of might.
Then look, what hate or any gall
Is tached[1] or tied thy limbs betwist ?
    Thy head hath neither greme nor grist[2]
    On arm or finger though thou bear ring.
    So fare we all with love and list[3]
    To King and Queen by Courtesy.

                        (From " Pearl

[1] Attached.   [2] Wrath nor spite.   Joy.

ANONYMOUS

(FOURTEENTH CENTURY)

Jonah

AS a mote in at a minster door, so mighty were its jaws,
Jonah enters by the gills, through slime and gore;
he reeled in through a gullet, that seemed to him a road,
tumbling about, aye head over heels,
till he staggers to a place as broad as a hall:
then he fixes his feet there and gropes all about,
and stands up in its belly that stank as the devil;
in sorry plight there, 'mid grease that savoured as hell
his bower was arrayed, who would fain risk no ill.
Then he lurks there and seeks in each nook of the navel
the best sheltered spot, yet nowhere he finds
rest or recovery, but filthy mire
wherever he goes; but God is ever dear.

(From " Patience.")

Quia amore langueo

IN a tabernacle of a tower,
  As I stood musing on the moon,
A crowned Queen, most of honour,
Appeared in ghostly sight full soon.
She made complaint thus by her own,
For man's soul was wrapped in woe:
" I may not leave mankind alone,
    Quia amore langueo.

I long for love of man my brother,
I am his vocate to void his voice;
I am his mother—I can none other—
Why should I my dear child despise ?
If he me wrath in diverse ways wise,
Through fleshes frailty fall me fro,
Yet must we rue him till he rise,
    Quia amore langueo

I bide, I bide in great longing,
I love, I look when man will crave.
I plain for pity of paining;
Would he ask mercy, he should it have.
Say to me, soul, and I shall save,
Bid me, my child, and I shall go;
Thou prayed me never but my Son forgave,
    Quia amore langueo.

ANONYMOUS

O wretch in the world, I look on thee,
I see thy trespass day by day,
With lechery against my chastity,
With pride against my poor array;
My love abideth, thine is away;
My love thee calleth, thou stealest me fro;
Sue to me, sinner, I thee pray,
          Quia amore langueo.

Mother of Mercy I was for thee made;
Who needeth it but thou alone?
To get the grace I am more glad
Than thou to ask it; why wilt thou none?
When said I nay, tell me to one?
Forsooth never yet to friend nor foe;
When thou askest nought, then make I moan,
          Quia amore langueo.

I seek thee in weal and wretchedness,
I seek thee in riches and poverty;
Thou man behold where thy mother is,
Why lovest thou me not sith I love thee?
Sinful or sorry however thou be,
So welcome to me there are none more;
I am thy sister, right trust on me,
          Quia amore langueo.

My child is outlawed for thy sin,
Mankind is better for his trespass;
Yet pricketh mine heart that so ny my kin
Should be disseased, o Son, alas!

Thou art his brother, his mother I was;
Thou sucked my pap, thou loved man so;
Thou died for him, mine heart he has,
   Quia amore langueo.

Man, leave thy sin then for my sake;
Why should I give thee that thou not would?
And yet if thou sin, some prayer take
Or trust in me as I have told.
Am not I thy mother called?
Why should I flee thee? I love thee so,
I am thy friend, I help, behold
   Quia amore langueo.

Now son, she said, wilt thou say nay,
When man would mend him of his miss?
Thou let me never in vain yet pray:
Then, sinful man, see thou to this,
What day thou comest, welcome thou is,
This hundreth year if thou were me fro—
I take thee full fain, I clip, I kiss
   Quia amore langueo

Now will I sit and say no more,
Leave and look with great longing,
When a man will call I will restore;
I love to save him, he is mine offspring;
No wonder if mine heart on him hang.
He was my neighbour; what may I do?
For him had I this worshipping,
   Quia amore langueo.

ANONYMOUS

Why was I crowned and made a queen ?
Why was I called of mercy the well ?
Why should an earthly woman been
So high in heaven above angel ?
For thee, mankind, the truth I tell;
Thou ask me help and I shall do
That I was ordained, keep thee from Hell,
　　　Quia amore langueo.

Now man, have mind on me for ever,
Look on thy love thus languishing;
Let us never from other dissever,
Mine help is thine own, creep under my wing
Thy sister is a queen, thy brother a king,
This heritage is tailed, soon come thereto,
Take me for thy wife and learn to sing,
　　　Quia amore langueo.

ANONYMOUS

(FOURTEENTH CENTURY)

Christ's Gift to Man

CHRIST maketh to man a fair present,
His bloody body with love brent;
That blissful body his life hath lent,
For love of man that sin hath blent.
O Love, Love what hast thou meant?
Me thinketh that love to wrath is went.

Thy mild bones love hath to-draw,
The nails thy feet have all to-gnaw;
The lord of love Love hath now slaw,
When Love is strong it hath no law.

That heart cleft for truth of love,
Therefore in him alone is true love;
For love of thee that heart is gove,
Keep thou that heart and thou art above.

Love hath showed his great might,
For Love hath made of day the night;
Love hath slaw the king of right,
And Love hath ended the strong fight.

Love, love where shalt thou won?
The woning-stead is thee be-nome,
For Christ's heart that was thine home;
He is dead, now thou hast none.
Love, love why dost thou so?
Love, thou breakest mine heart a two.

ANONYMOUS

King Arthur's Dream

THE Water-Lion is the God verray
  God to the Lion is likened many way;
The water was their own fragility
And their trespass and their iniquity
Into this world, the which they stand enclosed,
That was the water which they have supposed,
That hath their knowledge made so imperfite
Their sin and eke their world's great delight,
As cloudy water was evermore between,
That they the Lion perfitly hath not seen
But God the which that is the Sovereign Leech
Needeth no manner medicine to sech;
For there is no infirmity nor wound,
But as Him liketh all is whole and sound.
So can He heal infirmity of thought,
Which that no earthly medicine can nought;
This is His might that never more shall sin,
This is the Leech withouten medicine.
Now of the flower I will to thee discern,
This is the flower that hath the fruit etern,
This is the flower that fadeth for no shower;
This is the flower, of whom the fruit was born,
This us redeemed after that we were lorn;
This is the flower that ever springeth new,
This is th flower that changeth never hue;
This is the Virgin, this is the blessed flower
That Jesu bore, that is our Salvour
This flower unwemmed[1] of her Virginity
This is the flower of our felicity,

[1] Unspotted.

65

ANONYMOUS

This is the flower to whom we should exhort
This is the flower ceaseth not to support
In prayer, counsel and in business
Us caitiffs aye into our wretchedness.
She shall such counsel give one to the two,
The Lion and the Sovereign Leech also.

King Arthur's Death

"O GO again," said the King,
"For love and charity
And throw my sword into that river
That never I do it see."

The Duke to the river side he went
And the King's scabbard in threw he,
And still he kept Escalberd
For virtue's sake fair and free.

He came again to tell the King:
The King said: "Lukin, what did thou see?"
"Nothing, my liege," then said the Duke,
"I tell you certainly."

"O go again, Lukin," said the King,
"Or the one of us shall die."
Then the Duke to the riverside went
And the King's sword there threw he.

A hand and an arm did meet that sword
And flourished three times certainly.
He came again to tell the King,
But the King was gone from under the tree.

But to what place he could not tell,
For never after he did him see,
But he see a barge from the land go
And heard ladies howl and cry certainly.

ANONYMOUS

But whether the King was there or no
He knew not certainly,
The Duke walked by that River's side
Till a chapel there found he.

And a priest by the altarside there stood,
The Duke kneeled down there on his knee
And prayed the priests: " For Christ's sake
The rights of the Church bestow on me."

ANONYMOUS

Domine, quo vadis?

NOW wend we to the Palmalle—
  Domine, quo vadis? men it call,
Where Peter met with Jesu
And said, " Lord, whither wilt Thou ?"
Christ answered to Peter tho.
" Into Rome," he said, " I go,
Eft to die on Rood for thee:
Thou dreadest to die, Peter, for me."
" Lord," he said, " Mercy I cry,
To take my death I am ready."
There is a sign of His foot
On marblestone where He stood.

(Vernon MS.)

ANONYMOUS

Brown Robin's Confession

IT fell upon a Wodensday
Brown Robin's men went to sea;
But they saw neither moon nor sun
Nor starlight with their e'e.

" We'll cast kevels[1] us among,
See who the man may be."
The kevel fell on Brown Robin,
The master man was he.

" It is no wonder," said Brown Robin,
" Altho' I do not thrive;
For I murdered mine old father," says he ;
" I would he were yet alive.

" But tie me to a plank of wood
And throw me in the sea;
And if I sink ye may bid me sink,
If I swim just let me be."

They've tied him to a plank of wood
And thrown him in the sea;
He didna sink though they bade him sink,
He swimed and they bade let him be.

He hadna been into the sea
An hour but barely three,
Till by and came Our Blessed Ladie,
Her dear young Son her wi'.

[1] Lots.

ANONYMOUS

"Will ye gang to your men again ?
Or will ye gang wi' me ?
Will ye gang to the high heavens,
Wi' my dear Son and me ?"

"I winna gang to my men again,
For they would be feared at me;
But I would gang to the high heavens
Wi' thy dear Son and thee."

"It's for no honour ye did, Brown Robin,
It's for no good ye did to me;
But it's all for your fair confession
You've made upon the sea."

ANONYMOUS

Becket's Diadem

A NOTHER knight smote Saint Thomas in that self
wound,
And made him bow his face adown and look toward the
ground.
The third in that self stead thereafter him smote anon
And maked him loute[1] adown his face to the stone.
In that stead the fourth smote then the other hadden er
i-do
And the point of his sword brake in the marblestone ato.
Yet that ilk point at Canterbury the Monachus doth wite.
For honour of the holy man that there with was i-smite;
With thulk stroke he smote off the skull and eke the crown
That the brain full on the pavement all abroad there down.
That white brain was i-mengd[2] with the red blood there,
That color was well fair; to see they it reulich[3] were
All round it orn[4] about his head as it were a diadem
And all around where abouten it lay wharof men token
great game.[5]

(*From " The South English Legendary."*)

[1] Bend.   [2] Mingled.   [3] Rueful.   [4] Flow.   [5] Delight.

ANONYMOUS

The Murder of Saint Thomas of Kent

L ISTEN lordings both great and small,
  I will tell you a wonder tale :
How Holy Church was brought in bale
   cum magna injuria.

The greatest clerk in this land,
Thomas of Canterbury I understand :
Slain he was with wicked hand
   malorum potentia.

The knights were sent from Harry ye King,
That day they did a wicked thing :
Wicked men without leasing
   per regis imperia.

Before the altar he kneeled down,
And then they pared his crown
And stirred his brains up so down :
   optans coeli gaudia.

ANONYMOUS

The "Pater Noster"

OUR Father our all-wielding is,
   God let us never His mirthes miss.
        Lord, hallowed be Thy name.
In Heaven and earth Thy will
Be done and that is skill[1]
        Or else we been to blame.
Our each day's bread give us to-day
That we may trustily, when we shall away,
        To come to Thy Kingdom.
God keep us to our last ending,
Let never the fiend with false fending[2]
        Cumber us in no shame.

(From "The Lay-Folks' Mass Book.")

[1] Possible.   [2] Tempting.

ANONYMOUS

Carol : The Five Joys of the Virgin

MARY, for the love of thee
    Blithe and glad may we be,
And I shall sing as ye may see,
      Sua quinque gaudia.

The first Joy was sent to thee
When Gabriel greeted thee
And said Hail Mary in chastity,
      Officiaris gravida.

The second Joy was full good
When Christ took both flesh and blood
Without sorrow and changing of mood,
      Enixa est puerpera.

The third Joy was of great might
When Jesu was on the Rood dight,
Dead and buried in all men's sight,
      Surrexit die tertia.

The fourth Joy was without aye
When Jesu to Hell took the way
And with him come great array,
      Ad coeli palacia.

The fifth Joy was on Holy Thursday
Unto Heaven He took the way,
God and man, and so He is for aye,
      Ascendit super sidera.

75

Three Christmas Carols

I

A BABE is born all of a May
In the savasyoun[1] of us;
To them we singen both night and day,
Veni Creator spiritus !

At Bedlem, that blessed place,
The child of bliss born he was;
Him to serve go give us grace,
O lux beata trinitas !

There come three kinges out of the east
To worship the king that is so free,
With gold and myrrh and frankincense,
A solis ortus cardine.

The herds hearden an angel cry,
A merry song then sungen he;
Why arn ye so sore aghast ?
Jam ortus solis cardine.

The angel coming down with a cry
A fair song then sungen he
In the worship of that child,
Gloria tibi domine.

II

Man, be merry, I thee rede,
But beware what mirthes thou make;
Christ is clothed in thy weed
And He is made man for thy sake.

1 Salvation.

ANONYMOUS

He came from His father's seat,
Into this world to be thy make;[1]
Man beware how thou Him treat,
For He is made man for thy sake.

Look thou mercy ever cry,
Now and alway, rathe[2] and late;
And He will set thee wonder high,
For He is made man for thy sake.

III

This night there is a child born
That sprang out of Jesse's thorn,
We must sing and say theforn,
   Verbum Caro factum est.

Jesus is the child's name
And Mary mild is His dame,
All our sorrow shall turn to game,
   Verbum Caro factum est.

[1] Mate.   Early.

The Trinity

THE Father was and aye shall be
  And is withouten end;
The Son died upon the tree,
Our false foen to schend;
The Holy Ghost that maketh Three
That may us grace send:
All is one in Trinity
What way thou turn or wend.
I may say withouten boast
The Holy Book lieth never;
Father and Son and Holighost
Be with us now and ever !

(*Vernon MS.*)

ANONYMOUS

Temperance

WINE taken with excess,
As Scripture doth express,
Causeth great heaviness
    Unto the mind.

But they that take pleasure
To drink it with measure
No doubt a great treasure
    They shall it find.

Then give not a cherry
For cider nor perry;
Wine maketh man merry,
    Ye know well this.

Then put aside all wrath,
For David shewed us hath;
Vinum laetificat
    Cor hominis.

Now, ye that be present,
Laud God omnipotent,
That hath us given and sent
    Our daily food.

When through sin were slain
He sent His Son again
Us to redeem from pain
    By His sweet blood.

ANONYMOUS

And He is the true Vine
From whom distilled the wine
That bought your souls and mine.
  You know well this.

Then put aside all wrath,
For David shewed us hath;
Vinum laetificat
    Cor hominis.

(British Museum MS.)

ANONYMOUS

The Coming of Christ

I SAW Him with flesh all bespred—He came from East.
I saw Him with blood all bissed—He came from West.
I saw that many He with Him brought—He came from
South.
I saw that the world of Him ne rought—He came from
North.

"I come from wedlock as a sweet spouse
That have my wife with me in-nome.
I come from fight a staleworthe[1] knight
That mine foe have overcome.
I come from the cheping as a rich chapman
That mankind hath bought.
I come from an uncouth land as a sely pilgrim
That far hath sought."

(Merton College MS.)

[1] Stalwart.

ANONYMOUS

Holy Cross

STEADFAST Cross, among all other
Thou art a tree mickle of price,
In branch and flower such another
I ne wot none in wood nor rys.
Sweet be the nails
And sweet be the tree,
And sweeter be the burden that hangs upon thee.

(Merton College MS.)

ANONYMOUS

QUATRAINS

The Monks of Ely

MERRY sang the monks who in Ely fare
    When Canute the King came rowing there
—Row, knights, nearer to the land
And hear we the song of monken band.

Fortune

THE Lady Fortune is both friend and foe;
    Of poor she maketh rich, of rich poor also,
She turneth woe all into weal and weal all into woe,
Nor trusteth man to this weal, the wheel it turneth so.

Phantasy

ALL is phantom that we mid fare,
    Naked and poor hence we shall fare,
All shall be other man's that we for care,
But that we done for God's love have we no mair.

(Cambridge University MS.)

LAURENCE MINOT

(1300–1352?)

The Burgesses of Calais

L ISTEN now and ye may lere
　　All men the sooth may understand,
The knights that in Calais were
Come to Sir Edward sore weeping
In kirtle one and sword in hand,
And cried: Sir Edward, thine we are;
Do now, Lord, by law of land
Thy will with us for evermare.

The noble burgess and the best
Come unto him to have their hire;
The common people were full pressed
Ropes to bring about their swire:[1]
They said all: Sir Philip our sire,
And his son Sir John of France,
Has left us ligging in the mire
And brought us till this doleful dance.

Our horses that were fair and fat
Are eaten up each one bidene;[2]
Have we neither coney nor cat
That are not eaten and hounds keen—
All are eaten up full clean,
Is neither left bitch nor whelp.
That is well on our semblance seen
And they are fled that should us help.

[1] Neck.　　　　　[2] Already.

THOMAS OCCLEVE

(1370–1450)

To Chaucer

BUT well away, so is mine heart woe
That the honour of English tongue is dead
Of which I was wont have counsel and rede.
O master dear and father reverend,
My master Chaucer, flower of eloquence,
Mirror of fructuous entendment,
O universal father in science,
Alas, that thou thine excellent prudence
In thy bed mortal mightest not bequeath.
What ailed death? alas why would he slay thee?
O death, that didst no harm singular
In slaughter of him, but all this land it smarteth:
But natheless yet hast thou no power
His name to slay; his high vertue asterteth[1]
Unslain fro thee, which aye us lively hurteth,
With books of his ornate enditing,
That is to all this land enlumining.

[1] Escapeth.

JOHN LYDGATE, Priest

(1370–1451)

To the Virgin

QUEEN of Heaven, of Hell eke Emperess,
   Lady of this world, O very lodestar !
To mariners gainst all mortal distress
In their passage that they do not err;
Thy look of mercy cast down from so far
On all thy servants by chaste compassion,
Grant them good peace, save them from mortal war,
To thy five Joys that have devotion.

Celestial Cypress set upon Syon,
Highest Cedar of perfit holiness,
Carbuncle of charity and green emerald stone,
Whole and unbroken by virginal clearness;
O Sapphire, loupe[1] all swelling to repress
Of cankered sores and venomous feloun,[2]
In ghostly woundes be their governess
To thy five Joys that have devotion.

Yard of Aaron, gracious and benign,
Well of all grace and merciful pity,
Where the Holy Ghost list to close and sign
The crystal cloister of thy Virginity;
Balm of Engadi gainst all Infirmity,
Of folk that languish to tribulation,
Preserve and keep from all adversity
To thy five Joys that have devotion.

[1] Precious stone.   [2] Sore.

JOHN LYDGATE

Against Women's Fashions

GREATEST of virtues is humility
  As Solomon saith, son of sapience,
Most was accept unto the Deity:
Taketh heed hereof, giveth to his words credence.

How Maria, which had a preminence
Above all women, in Bedlem when she lay
At Christes birth, no cloth of great dispence,
She weared a coverchief, *horns were cast away*

Made stable in God by ghostly confidence
This Rose of Jericho, there grew none such in May
Poor in spirit, perfect in patience,
In whom *all horns of pride were put away.*

Was never clerk by rhetoric nor science,
Could all her virtues rehearse unto this day
Noble Princess of much benevolence
By example of her *your horns cast away.*

JAMES I OF SCOTLAND

(1394–1437)

Good Counsel

SINCE through vertue encreaseth dignity,
    And vertue flower and root is of noblay,[1]
Of any weal or what estate thou be,
    His steppis sew,[2] and dread thee non effray:
    Exile all vice, and follow truth alway:
Love most thy God, that first thy love began,
And for ilk inch he will thee quit a span.

Be not o'er proud in thy prosperity,
    For, as it comes, so will it pass away;
Thy time to compt is short, thou may well see,
    For of green grass soon cometh walowit[3] hay.
    Labour in truth while light is of the day.
Trust most in God, for he best guide thee can,
And for ilk inch he will thee quit a span.

Since word is thrall, and thought is only free,
    Thou dant[4] thy tongue that power has and may;
Thou steik[5] thine een fra worldis vanity;
    Refrain thy lust, and harken what I say;
    Graip or thou slide, and creep forth on the way;
Keep thy behest unto thy God and man,
And for ilk inch he will thee quit a span.

[1] Noblesse.	[2] Ensue.	[3] Withered
[4] Restrain.	[5] Hide.	

ROBERT HENRYSON

(1425–1500)

To Our Lady

O LADY leal and lovesomest,
   Thy face most fair and sheen is!
O blossom blithe and buxomest,
From carnal crime that clean is !
This prayer from my spleen is,
That all my works wickedest
Thou put away and make me chaste
From Termagent that teen[1] is
And from his claw that keen is;
And syne till heaven my soul thou hast
Where thy Maker of mightiness most
Is King and thou their Queen is !

[1] Grief.

ROBERT HENRYSON

The Garment of Good Ladies

OF high Honour should be her hood
    Upon her head to wear,
Garnished with Governance so good
No deeming should her dare.

Her sark[1] should be her body next
Of Chastity so white
With shame and dread together mixt
The same should be perfit.

Her kirtle should be of clean Constance
Laced with leasome Love,
The eyelets of Continuance
For never to remove.

Her belt should be of Benignity,
About her middle met;
Her mantle of Humility
To thole both wind and wet.

Her hat should be of fair having
And her tippet of truth;
Her patelet of good pansing,[2]
Her halse[3] ribbon of ruth.

Her sleeves should be of Esperance
To keep her from despair;
Her gloves of good Governance
To guide her fingers fair.

[1] Shirt.   [2] Thinking.   Neck.

Her shoon should be of sickerness[1]
In sign that she not slide;
Her hose of Honesty, I guess,
I should for her provide.

[1] Security.

JOHN SKELTON, Priest

(1460–1529)

The Gift of a Skull

YOUR ugly token
    My mind hath broken
From worldly lust.
For I have discussed
We are but dust
And die we must.
It is generall
To be mortall.
I have well espied
No man may him hide!
With sinews witheréd,
From death hollow-eyed.
With bones shudderéd
With his worm-eaten maw,
And his ghastly jaw.
Gasping aside,
Naked of hide,
Neither flesh nor fell.
Then by my counsel
Look that ye spell
Well this Gospell.
For whereso we dwell,
Death will us quell
And with us mell.
For all our pampered paunches
There may no fraunchise
For worldly bliss,
Redeem us from this,

JOHN SKELTON

Our days be dated,
To be check-mated,
With draughts of death
Stopping our breath,
Our eyen sinking,
Our bodies stinking,
Our gummys grinning,
Our souls brynning.
To whom then shall we sue
For to have rescue
But to sweet Jesu
On us then for to rue.
O goodly child
Of Mary Mild,
Then be our shield.
That we be not exiled
To the dyne dale
Of bottomless bale,
Nor to the lake
Of fiendys blake.
But grant us grace
To see thy face,
And to purchase
Thine heavenly place,
And thy palace
Full of solace
Above the sky,
That is so high.
Eternally
To behold and see
The Trinity. Amen.

JOHN SKELTON

The Funeral of Philip Sparrow

*K*YRIE *Eleison !*
   For Philip Sparrow's soul
Set in our bead roll
Let us now whisper
A *Pater Noster*
Lauda anima mea Dominum.
To weep with me look that ye come
All manner of birds in your kind,
See none be left behind,
Some to sing and some to say,
Some to weep and some to pray;
The goldfinch, the wagtail,
The jangling jay to rail,
The flecked pie to chatter
Of this dolorous matter;
And Robin redbreast
He shall be the priest
The requiem masses to sing,
Loftly warbeling
With help of the red sparrow
And the chattering swallow
This herse for to hallow,
And also the mad coot,
With a bald face to toot,
The raven called rolfe
His plaining to solfe;[1]

[1] Note in music.

94

JOHN SKELTON

The partridge, the quail,
The plover with us to wail;
The woodhack that singeth churr
Hoarsely as he had the murre,[1]
The lusty chanting nightingale,
The popinjay to tell her tale
That tooteth oft in a glass
Shall read the Gospel at Mass;
The mavis with her whistle
She rede there th' Epistle,
With peewit, the lapwing
The versicles shall sing;
The bittern with his bump,
The crane with his trump,
The duck and the drake
Shall watch at this wake.

*　　●　　●

Also the noble falcon
With the gyrfalcon,
The tircel gentle,
They shall mourn soft and still
In their amice of gray.
The *Sacre* with them shall say
Dirige for Philip's soul,
The goshawk shall have a roll
The choristers to control,
The lanners[2] and martins
Shall stand in their morning gowns,
The hobby and the musket
The censers and the cross shall set;

[1] Cold.　　　　[2] Hawks.

JOHN SKELTON

The kestrel in all this work
Shall be holy-water clerk.
And now the dark cloudy night
Chaseth away Phoebus bright,
Taking his course toward the west;
God send my sparrow's soul good rest.

JOHN SKELTON

(SIXTEENTH CENTURY)

To Mistress Margeret Hussey

MERRY Margeret
As midsummer flower,
Gentle as falcon
Or hawk of the tower;
With solace and gladness,
Much mirth and no madness,
All good and no badness;
So joyously,
So maidenly,
So womanly
Her demeaning
In everything,
Far, far passing
That I can indite,
Or suffice to write
Of Merry Margeret
As midsummer flower,
Gentle as falcon
Or hawk of the tower.
As patient and still
And as full of good will
As fair Isaphill,
Coliander,
Sweet pomander,
Good Cassander;
Steadfast of thought,
Well made, well wrought,
Far may be sought,

JOHN SKELTON

Ere that ye can find
So courteous, so kind,
As Merry Margeret,
This midsummer flower,
Gentle as falcon
Or hawk of the tower.

JOHN SKELTON

The Parrot

MY name is Parrot, a bird of Paradise,
By nature devised of a wonderous kind,
Daintily dieted with divers delicate spice,
Till Euphrates, that flood, driveth me into Ind;
Where men of that country by fortune me find,
And send me to great ladies of estate.
Then Parrot must have an almond or a date.

For Parrot is no churlish chough nor no flecked pie,
Parrot is no Pendugum[1] that men call a gairling,
Parrot is no woodcock nor no butterfly,
Parrot is no stammering stare, that men call a starling;
But Parrot is my own dear heart and my dear darling;
Melpomene, that fair maid, burnished his beak:
I pray you, let Parrot have liberty to speak.

Parrot is a fair bird for a lady;
God of his goodness him framed and wrought;
When Parrot is dead, she doth not putrefy:
Yea, all thing mortal shall turn into nought,
Except man's soul, that Christ so dear bought;
That never may die, nor never die shall:
Make much of Parrot, the Popejay royall.

For that Peerless Prince that Parrot did create
He made you of nothing by His majesty:
Point well this problem that Parrot doth prate,
And remember among how Parrot and ye
Shall leap from this life, as merry as we be;
Pomp, pride, honor, riches and worldly lust,
Parrot saith plainly shall turn all to dust.

[1] Penguin.

WILLIAM DUNBAR

(1465–1530)

Ballad of Our Lady

HAIL sterne[1] superne ! Hail in eterne
In Godis sight to shine !
Lucerne in dern,[2] for to discern
Be glory and grace divine;
Hodiern, modern, sempitern,
Angelical regine !
Our tern[3] inferne for to dispern,
Help royalest rosine.
Ave Maria Gratia plena !

Hail fresh flower feminine !
Yerne[4] us, guberne, virgin matern,
Of ruth both root and rine.
Hail, ying,[5] benign, fresh flourishing !
Hail, Alpha's habitacle !
The dign offspring made us to sing
Before his tabernacle;
All thing malign we down thing
By sight of His signacle;
Which King us bring unto His ring
Fro Death's dark umbracle.
Ave Maria Gratia plena !

Hail moder and maid but macle ![6]
Bright sign, glading our languishing,
By might of the miracle
Empress of price, imperatrice,
Bright polished precious stone;

1 Star.   2 Lamp in dark.   3 Trouble.
4 Move.   5 Young.   6 Without macula.

100

WILLIAM DUNBAR

Victrice of vice, high genetrice
Of Jesu, Lord Soverane:
Our wise paviss[1] fro enemies
Again the Fiend's train;
Oratrice, mediatrice, salvatrice
To God great suffragane !
   Ave Maria Gratia plena !

Hail sterne meridiane !
Spice, flower-de-lyce of paradise,
That bare the glorious grain.
Imperial wall, place palestral,
Of peerless pulchritude ;
Triumphal hall, high tower royal
Of Godis celsitude;
Hospital royal ! the Lord of all
Thy closet did include;
Bright ball crystal, rose virginal
Fulfilled of angel food !
   Ave Maria Gratia plena !

Thy birth has with His blood
Fro fall mortal original
Us ransomed on the Rood.

  1 Shield.

WILLIAM DUNBAR

Lament for the Makars[1]

I THAT in health was and gladness
  Am troubled now with great sickness
And feebled with infirmity:—
    Timor Mortis conturbat me.

Our pleasance here is all vain glory,
This false world is but transitory;
The flesh is bruckle,[2] the Fiend is slee:—
    Timor Mortis conturbat me.

The state of man does change and vary,
Now sound, now sick, now blythe, now sorry,
Now dancing merry, now like to die:—
    Timor Mortis conturbat me.

No state in Earth here standeth sicker;[3]
As with the wind waveth the wicker
So waneth this world's vanity:—
    Timor Mortis conturbat me.

Unto the Death goes all Estates,
Princes, Prelates, and Potestates,
Both rich and poor of all degree:—
    Timor Mortis conturbat me.

He takes the Knights into the field
Enarmed under helm and shield;
Victor he is at all mellie:—
    Timor Mortis conturbat me.

[1] Poets.   [2] Brittle.   [3] Sure.

WILLIAM DUNBAR

That strong unmerciful tyrant
Takes, on the mother's breast suckand,
The babe full of benignity:—
  Timor Mortis conturbat me.

He takes the champion in the stour,[1]
The captain closed in the tower,
The lady in bower full of beauty:—
  Timor Mortis conturbat me.

He spares no lord for his puissance,
No clerk for his intelligence;
His awful stroke may no man flee:—
  Timor Mortis conturbat me.

Art-magicians and astrologers,
Rhetors, logicians, and theologers,
Them helpeth no conclusions slee:—
  Timor Mortis conturbat me.

In medicine the most practicians,
Leeches, surgeons, and physicians,
Themselves from Death may not supplee:—[2]
  Timor Mortis conturbat me.

I see that Makars among the lave[3]
Play here their pageants, soon go to grave;
Spared is not their faculty:—
  Timor Mortis conturbat me.

He has done petuously devour
The noble Chaucer, of Makars flower.
The Monk of Bury, and Gower, all three:—
  Timor Mortis conturbat me.

  [1] Fight.   [2] Save.   [3] The rest.

WILLIAM DUNBAR

Since he has all my brothers ta'en,
He will not let me live alane;
Of force I must his next prey be:—
    Timor Mortis conturbat me.

Since for the Death remedy is none,
Best is it that we for Death dispone,
After our death that live may we:—
    Timor Mortis conturbat me.

GAVIN DOUGLAS, Bishop
(1474–1522)

Welcome to the Sun

WELCOME the lord of light, and lamp of day,
    Welcome foster of tender herbys green,
Welcome quickener of florist flowers sheen,[1]
Welcome support of every root and vein,
Welcome comfort of all kind fruit and grain,
Welcome the birdies bield[2] upon the briar,
Welcome master and ruler of the year,
Welcome welfare of husbands at the ploughs,
Welcome repairer of woods, trees and boughs,
Welcome depainter of the blooming meads,
Welcome the life of every thing that spreads,
Welcome stourer[3] of all kind bestial,
Welcome by thy bright beams, gladding all,
Welcome celestial mirror and espy![4]

(From the Prologue to " Æneid," xii.)

---

[1] Flourishing flowers bright.   [2] Nest   [3] Guardian.
[4] Sentinel.

STEPHEN HAWES

(1474 ?–1523 ?)

An Epitaph

O MORTAL folk, you may behold and see
How I lie here, sometime a mighty knight:
The end of joy and all prosperity
Is death at last, through his course and might:
After the day there cometh the dark night,
For though the day be never so long,
At last the bells ringeth to evensong.

STEPHEN HAWES

The True Knight

FOR knighthood is not in the feats of war,
  As for to fight in quarrel right or wrong,
But in a cause which truth can not defarre:[1]
He ought himself for to make sure and strong,
Justice to keep, mixt with mercy among:
And no quarrel a knight ought to take
But for a truth, or for a woman's sake.

For first good hope his Leg-Harness should be,
His Habergeon, of perfect righteousness
Gird fast with the Girdle of chastity.
His rich Placard should be good business
Broidered with alms so full of largess;
The Helmet, meekness, and the Shield, good faith,
His Sword God's word, as Saint Paul saith.

Also true widows he ought to restore
Unto their right, for to attain their dower;
And to uphold, and maintain evermore
The wealth of maidens, with his mighty power.
And to his sovereign at every manner hour
To be ready, true, and eke obeisant
In stable love fixt, and not variant.

(*From "The Pastime of Pleasure."*)

[1] Undo.

ALEXANDER BARCLAY, Priest

(1475-1552)

The Tudor Rose

(247) REMEMBER Richard, lately king of price,
　　In England reigning unrightwisely awhile,
How him ambition and guileful covetise
With innocent blood his hands did defile;
But howbeit that Fortune on him did smile
Two years or three, yet God sent him punishment
By his true servant: the Red Rose Redolent!

(From " The Ship of Fools.")

ALEXANDER BARCLAY

Preachment for Preachers

(333) YE clerks that on your shoulders bear the shield
    Unto you granted by the University,
How dare ye aventure to fight in Christes field
Against sin without ye clear and guiltless be?
Consider the cock and in him shall ye see
A great example, for with his winges thrice
He betides himself to wake his own body
Before he crow to cause others wake or rise.

(From " The Ship of Fools.")

ALEXANDER BARCLAY

Geographers

(1000) YE people that labour the world to measure
    Thereby to know the regions of the same,
Know first yourself; that knowledge is most sure,
For certainly it is rebuke and shame
For man to labour only for a name,
To know the compass of all the world wide
Not knowing himself nor how he should him guide.

(From " The Ship of Fools.")

ALEXANDER BARCLAY

Star of the Sea

(1972) THOU art the Star, blazing with beames bright
   Above these worldes waves so violent,
Our sins dark enclearing with thy light
Man's Mediatrice to God Omnipotent.
Wherefore to thee, O Lady, I present
This simple book, though it unworthy be,
But poor and simple and much ineloquent,
Rudely composed in this tempestuous sea.

       (From " The Ship of Fools."),

JOHN HEYWOOD

(1497–1580)

The Palmer

ST UNCUMBER and St Trumnion
    At St Botolph and St Anne of Buxton,
On the hills of Armenia where I saw Noe's Ark
With holy Job and St George in Southwark;
At Waltham and at Walsingham;
And at the good rood at Dagenham
At St Cornelys; at St James in Gales,
And at St Winifred's well in Wales;
At our Lady of Boston; at St Edmundsbury
And straight to St Patrick's Purgatory;
At Redburne and at the Blood of Hales
Where pilgrims' pains right much avails;
At St David's and at St Denis,
At St Matthew and St Mark in Venice,
At Master John Shorn at Canterbury,
The great God of Catwade, at King Henry,
At St Saviour's, at our Lady of Southwell,
At Crome, at Willesden and at Muswell;
At St Richard and at St Rock;
And at Our Lady that standeth in the Oak.

(*From "The Play of the Four P.P."*)

JOHN HEYWOOD

The English Schoolboy

ALL my pleasure is in catching of birds,
  And making of snowballs and throwing the same,
For the which purpose to have set in frame,
With my godfather good I would fain have spoken,
Desiring him to have sent me by some token
Where I might have had great frost for my pitfalls
And plenty of snow to make my snowballs.
This once had, boys' lives be such as no man leads.
O, to see my snowballs light on my fellows' heads,
And to hear the birds how they flicker their wings
In the pitfall! I say it passeth all things.

(*From " The Play of the Weather."*)

JOHN HEYWOOD

EPIGRAMS

1. *Tyburn and Westminster*

SUITS hang half a year in
Westminster Hall;
At Tyburn half an hour's
hanging endeth all.

2. *Cardinal Fisher* [1]

"SET he that Hat on his head?"
"Nay, chance so led
That by that time the Hat
came he had no head."

3. *The " Gloria Patri "*

"DICK, I marvel much why in every plat
Gloria Patri standeth before *Sicut erat*."
"Tom, *Gloria Patri* is a gentleman:
In pleasant speech, speak so sweetly no tongue can.
Sicut erat is a churl, so rude and plain
That to hear him speak all degrees do disdain."

[1] Martyred 1535.

ANONYMOUS

Medieval Mirth

THE Squire her hent in arms two
   And kissed her an hundred times and more.
There was mirth and melody,
With harp, gytron and sawtry,
With rote, ribible and clokard,
With pipes, organs and bombard,
With other minstrels them among,
With sytolph and with sawtry song,
With fiddle, record, and dulcimer,
With trumpet and with clarion clear,
With dulcet pipes of many cords
In chamber revelying all the lords
Unto morn that it was day.

(From " The Squire of Low Degree.")

The Kiss

MY ghostly father, I me confess,
First to God and then to you,

That at a window—wot ye how ?—
I stole a kiss of great sweetness,
Which done was out avisedness;
But it is done not undone now.
My ghostly father, I me confess,
First to God and then to you.

But I restore it shall doubtless
Again, if so be that I mow;
And that to God I make a vow
And else I ask forgiveness.
My ghostly father, I me confess,
First to God and then to you.

ANONYMOUS

" *O Felix Culpa !* "

ADAM lay inbounden
    Bounden in a bond;
Four thousand winter
Thought he not too long;
And all was for an apple,
An apple that he took
As clerics finden
Written in their book;
Nor had the apple taken been,
The apple taken been,
Nor had never Our Lady
Been of Heaven Queen.
Blessed be the time
That apple taken was.
Therefore we must singen
Deo Gratias.

Hugh of Lincoln

ALL the boys of merry Lincoln
Were playing at the ball,
And by it came him sweet Sir Hugh,
And he play'd o'er them all.

He kicked the ball with his right foot,
And catch'd it with his knee,
And through and through the Jew's window
He gar'd the bonny ball flee.

He's doen him to the Jew's castle,
And walk'd it round about;
And there he saw the Jew's daughter
At the window looking out.

' Throw down the ball, ye Jew's daughter,
Throw down the ball to me !"
" Never a bit," says the Jew's daughter,
" Till up to me come ye."

" How will I come ?   How can I come up ?
How can I come up to thee ?
I winna come up, I darena come up,
Without my play-fares three."

She's taken her to the Jew's garden,
Where the grass grew long and green,
She's pulled an apple red and white
To wile the pretty boy in.

She's wiled him in through a dark door,
And so has she through nine;
She's laid him on a dressing-table,
And stickit him like a swine.

And first came out the thick, thick blood,
And syne came out the thin,
And syne came out the bonny heart's blood:
There was no more within.

She's wrapped him in a cake of lead,
Bade him lie still and sleep;
She's thrown him into Our Lady's draw-well,
Was fifty fathom deep.

When bells were rung, and mass was sung,
And all the bairns came hame,
Then every lady had hame her son,
But Lady Helen had nane.

She's ta'en her mantle her about,
Her coffer by the hand,
And she's gone out to seek her son,
And wandered o'er the land.

She's doen her to the Jew's castle
Where all were fast asleep;
Cries, " Bonny Sir Hugh, O pretty Sir Hugh,
I pray you to me speak !"

She neared Our Lady's deep draw-well,
And fell down on her knee:
" Where'er ye be, my sweet Sir Hugh, .
I pray you speak to me !"

ANONYMOUS

" O the lead is wondrous heavy, mother,
The well is wondrous deep;
The little penknife sticks in my throat,
And I canna to ye speak.

" Go home, go home, my mother dear,
Prepare my winding sheet,
And at the back of merry Lincoln
The morn I will you meet."

Now Lady Helen is gone home,
Made him a winding sheet,
And at the back of merry Lincoln
The dead corpse did her meet.

And all the bells of merry Lincoln
Without men's hands were rung;
And all the books of merry Lincoln
Were read without man's tongue;
And never was such a burial
Since Adam's day begun.

The Maid and the Palmer

THE maid she went to the well to wash,
Dew fell off her lily-white flesh.

White she washed, and white she wrung,
White she hang'd on the hazel wand.

There came an old palmer by the way,
Says, " God speed thee well, thou fair may.

" Hast thou either cup or can,
To give an old palmer drink therein ?"

Says, " I have neither cup nor can,
To give an old palmer drink therein."

" But an thy leman[1] come from Rome,
Cups and cans thou wilt find soon."

She swore by God and good Saint John
Leman she had never none.

Says, " Peace, fair maid, you are foresworn,
Nine children have you borne.

" Three were buried under thy bed's head,
Other three under thy brewing lead.

" Other three play on yon green;
Count, maid, and there be nine."

" But I hope you are the good old man
That all the world believes upon.

---

[1] Sweetheart.

ANONYMOUS

"Old palmer, I pray thee,
Penance thou wilt give to me."

"Penance I can give thee none
But seven year to be a stepping-stone.

"Other seven a clapper in a bell,
Other seven to lead an ape in hell.

"When thou hast thy penance done,
Then thou'st come a maiden home."

The Friar of Orders Grey

IT was a Friar of Orders grey
  Walked forth to tell his beads;
And he met with a lady fair
Clad in a pilgrim's weeds.

" Now Christ thee save, thou reverend Friar,
I pray thee tell to me,
If ever at yon holy shrine
My true love thou didst see."

" And how should I know your true love
From many another one ?"
" O by his cockle hat and staff
And by his sandal shoon."

" O Lady, he is dead and gone ;
Lady, he's dead and gone,
And at his head a green grass turf
And at his heels a stone."

The Falcon

HE bare him up, he bare him down,
  He bare him into an orchard brown.
Lully, lulley, lully, lulley !
The falcon hath borne my Mate away.

In that orchard there was an hall,
That was hanged with purple and pall.

And in that hall there was a bed,
That was hanged with gold so red.

And in that bed there lieth a Knight,
His wounds bleeding day and night.

By that bedside kneeleth a May,
And she weepeth both night and day.

And by that bedside there standeth a stone,
" *Corpus Christi* " written thereon.
Lully, lulley, lully, lulley !
The falcon hath borne my Mate away.

ANONYMOUS

Two Carols to Our Lady

I

I SING of a maiden
That is makeless,[1]
King of all kings
To her son she chose.

He came all so still
There his mother was,
As dew in April
That falleth on the grass.

He came all so still
To his mother's bower,
As dew in April
That falleth on the flower.

He came all so still
There his mother lay,
As dew in April
That falleth on the spray.

Mother and maiden
Was never none but she;
Well may such a lady
God's mother be.

II

There is no rose of such virtue
As is the rose that bare Jesu.
    Alleluia.

For in this rose contained was
Heaven and earth in little space,
    Res miranda.

[1] Matchless.

ANONYMOUS

Be that rose we may well see
There be one God in persons three,
   Pares forma.

The angels sungen the shepherds to
Gloria in excelsis Deo.
      Gaudeamus.

Leave we all this worldly mirth,
And follow we this joyful birth
      Transeamus.

I Saw Three Ships

AS I sat under a sycamore tree,
    A sycamore tree, a sycamore tree,
I looked me out upon the sea
On Christ's Sunday at morn.

I saw three ships a-sailing there,
A-sailing there, a-sailing there,
Jesu, Mary and Joseph they bare
On Christ's Sunday at morn.

Joseph did whistle and Mary did sing,
Mary did sing, Mary did sing,
And all the bells on earth did ring
For joy our Lord was born.

O they sailed into Bethlehem !
To Bethlehem, to Bethlehem;
Saint Michael was the steersman,
Saint John sat in the horn.

And all the bells on earth did ring,
On earth did ring, on earth did ring:
" Welcome be thou Heaven's King,
On Christ's Sunday at morn !"

Two Old Lenten Rhymes

I

LENTEN stuff is come to the town,
   The cleansing week comes quickly;
You know well inow you must kneel down:
Come on, take ashes trickly.

Herring, herring, white and red,
Seek out such as be rotten;
Though some be hanged and some be dead
And some be yet forgotten.

Walfleet oysters salt and green
Are trim meats to be eaten:
Trusty subjects to their queen
Need never to be beaten.

Lily-white mussels have no peer,
The fishwives fetch them quickly:
So he that hath a conscience clear
May stand to his tackle trickly.

Carp is counted very good,
A trim fish and a dainty,
But if it smell once of the mud
Who'll give a groat for twenty?

Gudgeons make a goodly dish
For such cheese as be sickly;
And as yet is a foolish fish
And will be taken quickly.

ANONYMOUS

Then Jack-a-Lent comes jostling in,
With the headpiece of a herring,
And saith: " repent you of your sin,
For shame, sirs, leave your swearing."

And to Palm Sunday doth he ride,
With sprats and herrings by his side,
And makes an end of Lenten tide.

II

Lenton has brought us, as I understand,
Laus tibi Domine tied in a band:
He is come to the coast in the wanniand[1]
And Sir *Te Deum* is put out off the land:
     No nay:
     Now there is no more to make,
     But the devil his neck crack
     That has made us all the break
     With *Alleluia !*

Does not he for envy put all away,
Both eggs and collops and *Alleluia*,
Fritters and frummety he closes in clay,
And of all the days in the week he makes Friday.
     No doubt
     There is more to tell,
     But by Saint Michael,
     First ring his bell
     All England about.

[1] Curse.

ANONYMOUS

Farewell, *Alleluia*, with thy liberty,
The gentlest song that is or may be;
He that hath thee exiled out of the country
A dog's death might he die, I pray the Trinity,
     Certain,
       He was comfort of care
       And weal of well fare.
       I pray to Jesus that Mary bare
       Send us him again.

DRAMATIC

DRAMATIC

The Harrowing of Hell

JESUS:

*P*RINCIPES *portas tollite,*
    Undo your gates, ye Princes of pride,
Et introibit rex gloriae :
The King of bliss comes in this tide.

                    (JESUS *enters Hell.*)

SATAN:

    Out harrow.[1] What hirelot is he
    That says his Kingdom shall be cried ?

DAVID (*in Limbo*):

    That may thou in my Psalter see,
    For of this Prince I prophesied.
    I said that he should break
    Your bars and bands by name,
    And of your works take wreck:
    Now shall thou see the same.

JESUS:

    This stead shall stand no longer stoken:
    Open up and let my people pass.

DIABOLUS:

    Out behold our bailey broken
    And bursten are all our bands of brass !

BEELZEBUB:

    What then, is Limbo lorn ? Alas !

              1 Help !

JESUS:

> *Attollite portas, principes, vestras et*
> *elevamini portae eternales et*
> *introibit Rex Gloriae.*

RIBALD:

> Out harrow out ! What devil is he
> That calls him king over us all ?
> Hark, Beelzebub, come nigh,
> For hideously I heard him call.

BEELZEBUB:

> Honour ? Heard'st thou, hirelot, for what deed
> All earthly men to me are thrall ?
> The Lad that thou callest Lord-in-lede[1]
> He never had herborough,[2] house, nor hall.

JESUS:

> *Attollite portas principes,*
> Open up, ye Princes of pains sere,
> *Et elevamini eternales*
> Your endless gates that ye have here.

SATAN:

> What page is there that makes press
> And calls him King of us in fere ?

DAVID:

> Of Him cometh all this light
> That shineth in this bower,
> He is full fierce in fight,
> Worthy to win honour.

[1] Lord-in-the-flesh.   [2] Harbour.

DRAMATIC

JESUS:

Ye Princes of Hell, open your gate
And let my folk further gone:
A Prince of Peace shall enter thereat
Whither ye will or none.

RIBALD:

What art thou that speakest thus?

JESUS:

A King of Bliss that hight Jesus.

(Miracle Play.)

The Desertion of Beauty and Strength

EVERYMAN:

ALAS, I am so faint I may not stand,
My limbs under me do fold:
Friends, let us not turn again to this land,
Not for all the world's gold.
For into this cave must I creep
And turn to the earth and there to sleep.

BEAUTY:

What, into this grave? alas!

EVERYMAN:

Yea, there shall you consume more or less.

BEAUTY:

And what, should I smother here?

EVERYMAN:

Yea, by my faith and never more appear
In this world live no more we shall,
But in Heaven before the highest Lord of all.

BEAUTY:

I cross out all this; adieu by Saint John;
I take my cap in my lap and am gone.

EVERYMAN:

What, Beauty, whither will ye?

BEAUTY:

Peace, I am deaf: I look not behind me,
Not and thou would give me all the gold in thy chest.

EVERYMAN:

Alas, whereto may I trust?
Beauty goeth fast away and from me:
She promised with me to live and die.

DRAMATIC

STRENGTH:

> Everyman, I will thee also forsake and deny:
> Thy game liketh me not at all.

EVERYMAN:

> Why, then ye will forsake me all:
> Sweet Strength, tarry a little space.

STRENGTH:

> Nay, Sir. By the Rood of Grace,
> I will hie me from thee fast,
> Though thou weep till thy heart brast.

EVERYMAN:

> Ye would ever bide by me, ye said.

STRENGTH:

> Yea, I have you far enough conveyed:
> Ye be old enough, I understand,
> Your pilgrimage to take on hand;
> I repent me that I hither came.

EVERYMAN:

> Strength, you to displease I am to blame;
> Will you break promise that is debt?

STRENGTH:

> In faith, I care not:
> Thou art but a fool to complain,
> You spend your speech and waste your brain:
> Go thrust thee into the ground.

EVERYMAN:

> I had went surer I should you have found.
> He that trusteth in his strength
> She him deceiveth at the length.
> Both Strength and Beauty forsaketh me,
> Yet they promised me fair and lovingly.

(From " Everyman.")

DRAMATIC

The Lament of Eve

L ORD ! when Thou wentest from this place,
   A worm with an angel's face,
He hyth[1] us to be full of grace
            The fruit if that we eat.
I did his bidding, alas, alas !
Now we be bounden in death's lace,[2]
I suppose it was Satanas
            To pain he gan us pete.[3]

Alas ! alas ! and wel away
That ever touched I the tree,
I wend as wretch in wealsome way,
In black bushes my bower shall be.
In Paradise is plenty of play,
Fair fruits right plenty,
The gates be shut with Goddes key,
My husband is lost because of me.
            Lieve spouse, now thou fonde.
Now stumble sore on stalk and stone,
My wit away is from me gone,
Wrythe on to my neckbone
            With hardness of thine honde.

Alas that ever we wrought this sin,
Our bodily sustenance for to win,
Ye must delve and I shall spin
            In care to ledyn our life.

(Miracle Play.)

1 Promised.   2 Web.   3 Pitch.

DRAMATIC

Satan and Pilate's Wife

SATAN:

OUT, out, harrow! Into bale am I brought.
  This bargain may I ban,
But if I work some wile, in woe must I won.[1]
This gentleman Jesu, of cursedness He can.
By any sign that I see, this same is God's Son.
And He be slain, our solace will cease.
He will save man's soul from our sonde,[2]
And reave us the remys[3] that are round.
I will on stiffly in this stound[4]
Unto Sir Pilate's wife, pertly and put me in press.[5]

O woman, be wise and ware, and won in thy wit.
There shall a gentleman Jesu unjustly be judged
Before thy husband in haste, and with hirelots be hight
And that doughty[6] to-day to death thus be dighted.
Sir Pilate for His preaching and thou
With need shall ye be namely[7] be noyed,
Your striff and your strength shall be stroyed.

(Miracle Play.)

[1] Dwell.	[2] Power.	[3] Kingdoms.	[4] Stead.
[5] Near.	[6] Good man.	[7] Especially.	

139

POLITICAL

THOMAS PHILIPPS, Priest

The Peace of the Roses

" THE rose, it is a royal flower."
 " The red or the white ? show his colour."
" Both be full sweet and of like savour."
" All one they be
That day to see
It liketh well me.
I love, I love, and whom love ye ?"

" I love the rose both red and white."
" Is that your pure perfect appetite ?"
" To hear talk of them is my delight."
" Joyed may we be
Our prince to see
And roses three.
Now have I loved, and whom love ye ?"
" I love a flower of fresh beauty."
" I love another as well as ye."
" That shall be proved here anon
If we three can agree in one."

WILLIAM FORREST, Priest
(1510–1565)

The Marigold

TO Mary our Queen, that flower so sweet,
    This Marigold I do apply,
For that the name doth serve so meet
And properly in each party;
For her enduring patiently
The storms of such as list to scold
At her doings, with cause why
Loth to see spring this Marigold.

Christ save her in her high estate
Therein in rest long to endure:
Christ so all wrongs here mitigate
That all may be to His pleasure:
The high, the low, in due measure
As members true with her to hold,
So each to be th' other's treasure
In cherishing the Marigold.

Be Thou, O God, so good as thus
Thy perfect faith to see take place,
Thy peace Thou plant here among us
That error may go hide his face:
So to concord us in each case
As in thy court it is enrolled,
We all as one to love Her Grace
That is our Queen, the Marigold.

The Wreck of Walsingham

IN the wrecks of Walsingham
   Whom should I choose,
But the Queen of Walsingham
To be guide to my muse?
Then, thou Prince of Walsingham,
Grant me to frame
Bitter plaints to rue thy wrong,
Bitter woe for thy name.

Bitter was it, oh, to see
The silly sheep
Murdered by the ravening wolves,
While the shepherds did sleep.
Bitter was it, oh, to view
The sacred vine,
While the gardeners played all close,
Rooted up by the swine.
Bitter, bitter, oh, to behold
The grass to grow
Where the walls of Walsingham
So stately did show.

Such were the works of Walsingham,
While she did stand:
Such are the wrecks as now do show
Of that holy land.
Level, level with the ground
The towers do lie,
Which, with their golden glittering tops,
Pierced once to the sky,

F

ANONYMOUS

Where were gates, no gates are now:
The ways unknown
Where the press of peers did pass,
While her fame far was blown.
Owls do shriek, where the sweetest hymns
Lately were sung:
Toads and serpents hold their dens,
Where the palmers did throng.

Weep, weep, O Walsingham,
Whose days are nights:
Blessings turned to blasphemies,
Holy deeds to despites;
Sin is where our Lady sate;
Heaven turned is to hell:
Satan sits where our Lord did sway—
Walsingham, oh, farewell.

(Rawl. MS. Poet. 242.)

ANONYMOUS

The Rising in the North

L ISTEN, lively lordings all,
Lithe and listen unto me,
And I will sing of a noble earl,
The noblest earl in the north countrie.

Earl Percy is into his garden gone,
And after him walks his fair ladie:
I heard a bird sing in mine ear,
That I must either fight or flee.

But come thou hither, my little foot-page,
Come thou hither unto me,
To master Norton thou must go
In all the haste that ever may be.

Commend me to that gentleman,
And bear this letter here fro me;
And say that earnestly I pray,
He will ride in my companie.

And when the letter it was read
Affore that goodly company,
I wis, if you the truth would know,
There was many a weeping eye.

Come you hither, my nine good sons,
Gallant men I trow you be:
How many of you, my children dear,
Will stand by that good earl and me?

Eight of them did answer make,
Eight of them spake hastilie,
O father, till the day we die
We'll stand by that good earl and thee.

Gramercy now, my children dear,
You show yourselves right bold and brave;
And whethersoe'er I live or die,
A father's blessing you shall have.

But what say'st thou, O Francis Norton,
Thou art mine eldest son and heir :
Somewhat lies brooding in thy breast;
Whatever it be, to me declare.

Father, you are an aged man,
Your head is white, your beard is grey;
It were a shame at these your years
For you to rise in such a fray.

Now fie upon thee, coward Francis,
Thou never learnedst this of me:
When thou wert young and tender of age,
Why did I make so much of thee ?

But, father, I will wend with you,
Unarm'd and naked will I be;
And he that strikes against the crown,
Ever an ill death may he dee.

Then rose that reverend gentleman,
And with him came a goodly band
To join with the brave Earl Percy,
And all the flower o' Northumberland.

ANONYMOUS

With them the noble Nevill came,
The earl of Westmoreland was he:
At Wetherby they mustered their host,
Thirteen thousand fair to see.

Lord Westmoreland his ancyent[1] raised,
The Dun Bull he raised on high,
And three Dogs with golden collars
Were there set out most royally.

Earl Percy there his ancyent spread,
The Half-Moon shining all so fair:
The Nortons ancyent had the cross,
And the five wounds our Lord did bear.

(From the " Percy Reliques.")

[1] Ensign.

ANONYMOUS

A Ballad of the Rising in the North

THE widows be woeful whose husbands be taken
The children lament them that are so forsaken,
The Churchmen they chanted the morrow mass bell,
Their pardons be granted, they hang very well.

Well-a-day, well-a-day, well-a-day, woe is me,
Sir Thomas Plumtre is hanged on a tree.

It is known they be fled that were the beginners,
It is time they were dead, poor sorrowful sinners;
For all their great haste they are hedged at a stay
With weeping and wailing to sing well-a-day.

Yet some hold opinion, all is well with the highest,
They are in good safety where freedom is nighest;
Northumberland need not be doubtful, some say,
And Westmoreland is not yet brought to the bay;

Where be the fine fellows that carried the crosses ?
Where be the devisers of idols and asses ?
Where be the gay banners were wont to be borne ?
Where is the devotion of gentle John Shorne ?

You shall have more news ere Candlemas come;
There be matters diffuse, yet looked for of some;
Look on and look still, as you long to hear news,
I think Tower Hill will make you all muse.

God prosper Her Highness and send her His Peace
To govern good people with grace and increase;
And send the deservers that seek the wrong way
At Tyburn some carvers to sing well-a-day.

Well-a-day, well-a-day, well-a-day, woe is me,
Sir Thomas Plumtre is hanged on a tree.

(*From " Elizabethan Broadsides."*)

THE MARTYRS

BLESSED THOMAS MORE

(MARTYRED 1535)

Consider Well

CONSIDER well that both by night and day
  While we busily provide and care
For our disport, our revel and our play,
For pleasant melody and dainty fare,
Death stealeth on full slily; unaware
He lieth at hand and shall us all surprise,
We wot not when nor where nor in what wise.

When fierce temptations threat thy soul with loss
Think on His Passion and the bitter pain,
Think on the mortal anguish of the Cross,
Think on Christ's blood let out at every vein,
Think of His precious heart all rent in twain;
For thy redemption think all this was wrought,
Nor be that lost which he so dearly bought.

BLESSED THOMAS MORE

To Fortune

MY flattering fortune, look thou never so fair,
    Or never so pleasantly begin to smile,
As though thou wouldst my ruin all repair,
During my life thou shalt me not beguile.
Trust shall I God, to enter in awhile
His haven of heaven sure and uniform,
Ever after thy calm, look I for a storm.
Long was I, Lady Luck, your serving man,
And now have lost again all that I got,
Wherefore when I think on you now and then,
And in my mind remember this and that,
Ye may not blame me though I beshrew
But in faith I bless you again a thousand times,
For lending me now some leisure to make rhymes.

(Written in the Tower of London)

VENERABLE PHILIP HOWARD

(DIED IN THE TOWER, 1595)

Hymn

O CHRIST, the glorious Crown
Of virgins that are pure;
Who dost a love and thirst for Thee
Within their minds procure;
Thou art the spouse of those
That chaste and humble be,
The hope, the life, the only help
Of such as trust in Thee.

All charity of those
Whose souls Thy love doth warm;
All simple pleasures of such minds
As think no kind of harm;
All sweet delights wherewith
The patient hearts abound,
Do blaze Thy name, and with Thy praise
They make the world resound.

The sky, the land, the sea,
And all on earth below,
The glory of Thy worthy Name
Do with their praises show.
The winter yields Thee praise,
And summer doth the same,
The sun, the moon, the stars and all
Do magnify Thy name.

155

VENERABLE PHILIP HOWARD

The roses that appear
So fair to outward sight;
The violets with their scent
Do yield so great delight;
The pearls, the precious stones,
The birds, Thy praise do sing,
The woods, the wells, and all delights,
Which from this earth do spring.

What creature, O sweet Lord,
From praising Thee can stay?
What earthly thing but, filled with joy,
Thine honour doth bewray?
Let us, therefore, with praise
Thy mighty works express,
With heart and hand, with mind, and all
Which we from Thee possess.

(From the Arundel Hymns.)

CHIDIOCK TICHBORNE

(MARTYRED 1586)

Retrospect

MY prime of youth is but a frost of cares,
  My feast of joy is but a dish of pain,
My crop of corn is but a field of tares,
And all my good is but vain hope of gain.
The day is past, and yet I saw no sun,
And now I live, and now my life is done.

The spring is past, and yet it hath not sprung;
The fruit is dead, and yet the leaves are green;
My youth is gone, and yet I am but young;
I saw the world, and yet I was not seen;
My thread is cut, and yet it is not spun,
And now I live, and now my life is done.

I sought my death, and found it in my womb;
I looked for life, and saw it was a shade;
I trod the earth, and knew it was my tomb;
And now I die, and now I am but made.
The glass is full, and now my glass is run,
And now I live, and now my life is done.

(Written in the Tower of London.)

HENRY WALPOLE, Jesuit

(MARTYRED 1595)

Martyrdom of Father Campion

ENGLAND look up ! Thy soil is stained with blood,
   Thou hast made martyrs many of thine own,
If thou hadst Grace, their deaths would do thee good.
The seed will take, which in such blood is sown,
And Campion's learning fertile so before,
Thus watered too, must needs of force be more.

All Europe wonders at so rare a man,
England is filled with rumour of his end.
London must needs, for it was present then
When constantly three saints their lives did spend,
The streets, the stones, the steps, they hale them by,
Proclaim the cause, for which these martyrs die.

The Tower says, the truth he did defend,
The Bar bears witness of his guiltless mind,
Tyburn doth tell, he made a patient end.
In every gate his martyrdom we find.
In vain you wrought, that would obscure his name,
For heaven and earth will still record the same.

His quartered limbs shall join with joy again,
An l rise a body brighter than the sun,
Your bloody malice tormented him in vain,
For every wrench some glory hath him won.
A ad every drop of blood, which he did spend,
Hath reaped a joy, which never shall have end.

158

VENERABLE JOHN THEWLIS, Priest

(MARTYRED 1616)

The Song of a Happy Rising

TRUE Christian hearts cease to lament,
    for grief it is in vain,
For Christ you know was well content
    to suffer bitter pain
That we may come to heaven's bliss,
    there joyfully to sing.
Who doth believe shall never miss
    to have a joyful rising !

But, England, here my heart is sad
    for thy great cruelty
And loss of faith which once thou had
    of Christianity.
In thee false doctrine doth appear
    abundantly to spring,
Which is the cause, I greatly fear,
    thou lose thy happy rising !

As for myself, I am not afraid
    to suffer constantly,
For why ? due debt must need be paid
    unto sweet God on high.
Saint Paul, he being firm of faith,
    hoping with saints to sing,
Most patiently did suffer death.
    Lord, send us happy rising !

VENERABLE JOHN THEWLIS

Mark well my ghostly victory,
   my friends both great and small;
Be firm of faith, remember me
   and dread not of your fall;
For you my sheep I shepherd have
   made labour for to bring
You to my fold, your souls to save.
   Christ, send us happy rising!

I have said Mass and Matins both
   and true Instructions taught,
Confirmed by the Holy Ghost
   and mighty power wrought;
The Holy Communion also
   with manna ever living,
The Holy Sacraments I taught.
   Lord, send us happy rising!

Christ's passion oft before your face
   I have declared plain,
How for our sins he suffered death
   and how he rose again ;
And how the twelve Apostles eke
   were put to death for preaching
The Catholic faith which Christ did teach
   Christ, send us happy rising!

The saints also did suffer death,
   and martyrs, as you hear,
And I myself am now at hand,
   but death I do not fear.

Then have I trust of greater grace
    unto my soul will bring,
When we shall meet both face to face
    before One heavenly King.

No hurdle hard nor hempen rope
    can make me once afraid,
No tyrant's knife against my life
    shall make me disamayed.
Though flesh and bones be broken and torn,
    my soul I trust will sing
Amongst the glorious company
    with Christ our heavenly King.

Thus I your friend John Thewlis
    have made my latest end,
Desiring God when his will is
    us all to heaven send,
Where neither strange nor damned crew
    can grief unto us bring,
And now I bid my last adieu.
    Christ, send us happy rising!

                        (Brit. Mus. Add. MS. 15225.)

A Song of Four Priests who Suffered
Death at Lancaster[1]

IN this our English coast much blessed blood is shed,
Two hundred priests almost in our time martyred
And many laymen die with joyful sufferance,
Many more in prison lie, God's cause for to advance.

Amongst this gracious troop that follow Christ his train,
To cause the Devil stoop four priests were lately slain;
Nutter's bold constancy with his sweet fellow Thwinge,
Of whose most meek modesty Angels and saints may sing.

Hunt's haughty courage stout with godly zeal so true;
Mild Middleton, O what tongue can half thy virtue show?
At Lancaster lovingly these martyrs took their end
In glorious victory, true faith for to defend.

And thus hath Lancashire offered her sacrifice
To daunt their lewd desire, and please our Saviour's eyes,
For by this means I trust truth shall have victory
When as that number just of such saints complete be.

Who the Holy Ghost doth move unto his deity
In fervent flames of love thus sacrificed to be,
Whose faith and fortitude, whose grace and constancy
With mildness meek indeed confoundeth heresy.

Whose sacred members rent and quarters set on high
Caused more to be content in the same cause to die,
Whose lives while they did live, whose blessed deaths also
Do admonition give what way we ought to go.

[1] Robert Nutter and Edward Thwinge martyred in 1600; Thurstan
Hunt and Robert Middleton in 1601.

If we should them despise, as many wretches do,
We should contemn likewise Our Blessed Saviour too.
Let their examples then move our hearts to relent:
These were most blessed men whom God to us hath sent.

God's holy truth they taught and sealed it with their blood,
Dying with torments fraught and all to do us good,
Let lying heresy with her false libels lout,[1]
Truth will have victory, through such mild champions stout

Praise be to God's good will, Who doth his truth defend;
Lord, to thy vineyard still such worthy workmen send,
And, Good Lord, grant us grace that we may constant be,
With our Cross in each place to please thy majesty.

(*Brit. Mus. Add. MS.* 15225.)

[1] Bend.

ANONYMOUS

A Prisoner's Song of Jerusalem

MY thirsty soul desires her drought
  at heavenly fountains to refresh;
My prisoned mind would fain be out
  of chains and fetters of the flesh.

The Under Song

Jerusalem, thy joys divine
  no joys may be compared to them,
No people blessed so as thine,
  no city like Jerusalem.
She looketh up unto her state
  from whence she down by sin did slide;
She mourns the more the good she lost,
  for present ill she doth abide.

She longs from rough and dangerous seas
  to harbour in the haven of bliss,
Where safety anchoreth at her ease
  and shore of sweet contentment is.
From banishment she more and more
  desires to see her country dear;
She sits and sends her sighs before,
  her joys and treasures all be there.

From Babylon she would return
  unto her home and town of peace,
Jerusalem, where joys abound
  continue still and never cease.

ANONYMOUS

There blustering winter never blows
    nor summer's parching heat doth harm;
It never freezes there nor snows,
    the weather ever temperate warm.

The trees do blossom, bud and bear;
    the birds do ever chirping sing;
the fruit is mellow all the year,
    they have an everlasting spring;
The pleasant gardens ever keep
    their herbs and flowers fresh and green;
All sorts of pleasant dainty fruits
    at all times there are to be seen.

The lily white, the ruddy rose,
    the crimson and carnation flowers,
Be watered there with honey dews
    and heavenly drops of golden showers;
Pomegranate, prince of fruit, the peach,
    the dainty date and pleasant fig,
The almond, muscatel and grape,
    exceeding good and wondrous big;

The lemon, orange, medlar, quince,
    the apricot and Indies spice,
The cherry, warden plum, and pear
    more sorts than were in Paradise;
The fruit more eyesome, toothsome far
    than that which grew on Adam's tree,
With whose delights assailed were
    and both suppressed Eve and he.

ANONYMOUS

The swelling odoriferous balm
    most sweetly there doth sweat and drop;
The fruitful and victorious palm
    lays out her mounty lofty top ;
The river wine most pleasant flows,
    more pleasant than the honeycomb,
Upon whose banks the sugar grows
    enclosed in reeds of cinnamon.

The walls of jasper stone be built,
    most rich and fair that ever was ;
The streets and houses paved and gilt
    with gold more clear than crystal glass ;
Her gates in equal distance be
    and each a glistering margarite,
Which comers-in far off may see,
    a gladsome and a glorious sight.

Her inward chambers of delight
    be decked with pearl and precious stone ;
The doors and posterns all be white
    of wrought and burnished ivory bone ;
Her sun doth never eclipse nor cloud,
    her moon doth never there wax wan;
The Lamb with light hath her endowed
    Whose glory pen cannot explain.

The glorious saints there dwellers be
    in number more than man can think,
So many in a company
    as love in likeliness doth think ;

ANONYMOUS

The stars in brightness they do pass
   in swiftness arrows from a bow,
In strength and fierceness steel and brass,
   in lightness fire, in whiteness snow.

Their clothing is more soft than silk,
   with girdles girt of beaten gold;
They in their hands more white than milk
   of palm triumphant branches hold;
Their faces shining like the sun
   shoot out their gladsome glorious beams.
The field is fought, the battle won;
   their heads be crowned with diadems.

Reward as merit different is,
   distinct their joy and happiness,
But each in joy of other's bliss
   Doth as his own the same possess;
So each in glory doth abound
   and all their glories do excel,
But whereas all to each redound,
   who can the exceeding glory tell?

Triumphant martyrs you may hear
   recount their dangers which do cease,
And noble citizens ever wear
   their happy gowns of joy and peace.
There learned clerks with sharpened wits
   their Maker's wondrous works do tell;
The judges grave on bench do sit
   to judge the tribes of Israel.

ANONYMOUS

The glorious courtiers ever there
    attend on person of their King,
With Angels joined in a choir
    melodious hymns of praises sing;
The virgin chaste in lily white,
    the martyrs clad in scarlet red,
The holy fathers which did write
    wear laurel garlands on their heads.

Each Confessor a golden crown
    adorned with pearl and precious stone;
The apostles pearls in renown
    like princes sit in regal throne;
Queen Mother Virgin immanent,
    than Saints and Angels more divine,
Like sun amidst the firmament
    above the planets all doth shine.

The King that heavenly palace rules
    doth bear upon his golden shield,
A cross in sign of triumph gules
    erected in a verdant field.
His glory saith as doth behoove
    him in his manhood for to take,
Whose godhead earth and heaven above
    and all that dwell therein did make.

Like friends all partners as in bliss
    with Christ their lord and master dear;
Like spouses they the bridegroom kiss,
    who feasteth them with heavenly cheer

With tree of life and manna sweet,
   which tasted doth such pleasure bring
As none to judge thereof be meet
    but such as banquet with the King.

With Cherubim their wings they move
   and mount in contemplation high ;
With Seraphim they burn in love,
   the beams of glory be so nigh.
The Virgin's children dear they be
   her loving Son for to embrace,
And Jesus his brethren for to see
   his Heavenly Father's glorious face.

O sweet aspect, vision of peace,
   happy regard and heavenly sight !
O endless joy without surcease,
   perpetual day which hath no night !
O well and wale fountain of life,
   offspring of everlasting bliss !
Eternal sun, resplendent light,
   and eminent cause of all that is !

River of pleasure, sea of delight,
   garden of glory evergreen !
O glorious glass and mirror bright
   wherein all truth is ever seen !
O princely palace, royal court,
   monarchal seat, imperial throne,
Where King of kings and Sovereign Lord
   for ever ruleth all alone !

ANONYMOUS

Where all the glorious saints do see
   the secrets of the Deity,
The godhead and in persons three
   the super-blessed Trinity;
The depth of wisdom most profound,
   all puissant high sublimity,
The breadth of love without all bound
   in endless long eternity.

The heavy earth below by kind
   above ascends the mounting fire:
Be this the centre of my mind
   and lofty sphere of her desire.
The chased deer do take the soil,
   the tired hart the thick and wood:
Be this the comfort of my toil,
   my refuge, hope and sovereign good.

The merchant cuts the seas for gain,
   the soldier serves for his renown,
The tillman[1] ploughs the grounds for grain:
   be this my joy and lasting crown.
The falconer seeks to see a flight,
   the hunter beats to see his game:
Long thou, my soul, to see that sight
   and labour to enjoy the same.

No hour without some one delight
   which he endeavours to attain:
Seek thou, my soul, both day and night
   this one which ever shall remain—

[1] Labourer.

170

This one contains all pleasure true ;
    all other pleasures are but vain.
Bid thou the rest, my soul, adieu,
    and seek alone this one to gain.

Go count the grass upon the ground
    or sands that be upon the shore,
And when you have the number found
    the joys thereof be many more—
More thousand thousand years they last
    and lodge within the happy mind,
And when so many years be past
    Yet more and more be still behind.

Far more they be than we can ween ;
    they do our judgement much excel.
No ear hath heard nor eye hath seen,
    no pen can write, no tongue can tell ;
An Angel's tongue cannot recite
    the endless joys of heavenly bliss
Which being wholly infinite
    beyond all speech and writing is.

We can imagine but a shade;
    it never entered into thought
What joy He is enjoyed that made
    all joy and them that joy of nought.
My soul cannot the joys contain;
    let her, Lord, enter into them,
For ever with thee to remain
    Within thy town Jerusalem.

                 (Brit. Mus. Add. MS. 15225.)

ROBERT SOUTHWELL, Jesuit

(MARTYRED 1595)

The Burning Babe

A S I in hoary Winter's night
    Stood shivering in the snow,
Surprised I was with sudden heat,
    Which made my heart to glow;
And lifting up a fearful eye
    To view what fire was near,
A pretty Babe, all burning bright,
    Did in the air appear;
Who, scorchèd with exceeding heat,
    Such floods of tears did shed,
As though His floods should quench His flames,
    Which with His tears were fed.
" Alas !" quoth He, " but newly born,
    In fiery heats I fry;
Yet none approach to warm their hearts
    Or feel My fire but I.
My faultless breast the furnace is,
    The fuel, wounding thorns,
Love is the fire, and sighs the smoke,
    The ashes, shames and scorns.
The fuel Justice layeth on,
    And Mercy blows the coals,
The metal in this furnace wrought
    Are men's defilèd souls,
For which, as now on fire I am
    To work them to their good,
So will I melt into a bath
    To wash them in My blood."

With this He vanished out of sight,
    And swiftly shrunk away;
And straight I callèd unto mind
    That it was Christmas Day.

The Martyrdom of Mary, Queen of Scots

GOD'S spice I was, and pounding was my due,
    In fading breath my incense savoured best;
Death was my mean my kernel to renew,
By lopping shot I up to heavenly rest.

Some things more perfect are in their decay,
Like spark that going out gives clearest light;
Such was my hap whose doleful dying day
Began my joy and termèd Fortune's spite.

Alive a Queen, now dead I am a Saint;
Once Mary[1] called, my name now Martyr is;
From earthly reign debarrèd by restraint,
In lieu whereof I reign in heavenly bliss.

My scaffold was the bed where ease I found,
The block a pillow of eternal rest;
My headman cast me in a blissful swound,
His axe cut off my cares from cumberd breast.

(*Brit. Mus. Add. MS.* 10422.)

[1] Inserted by a different hand in the MS.

173

ROBERT SOUTHWELL

Times go by Turns

THE loppèd tree in time may grow again,
   Most naked plants renew both fruit and flower ;
The sorriest wight may find release of pain,
   The driest soil suck in some moistening shower;
Times go by turns, and chances change by course,
From foul to fair, from better hap to worse.

The sea of Fortune doth not ever flow;
   She draws her favours to the lowest ebb;
Her tide hath equal times to come and go;
   Her loom doth weave the fine and coarsest web;
No joy so great but runneth to an end,
No hap so hard but may in time amend.

Not always fall of leaf nor ever spring,
   No endless night, yet not eternal day;
The saddest birds a season find to sing,
   The roughest storm a calm may soon allay:
Thus with succeeding turns God tempereth all,
That man may hope to rise, yet fear to fall.

A chance may win that by mischance was lost;
   The net that holds no great, takes little fish;
In some things all, in all things none are cross'd,
   Few all they need, but none have all they wish;
Unmingled joys here to no man befall:
Who least, hath some; who most, hath never all.

ROBERT SOUTHWELL

Love's Servile Lot

SHE makes thee seek, yet fear to find,
  To find but not enjoy;
In many frowns some gliding smiles
She yields, to more annoy.

She woos thee to come near her fire,
Yet doth draw it from thee;
Far off she makes thy heart to fry,
And yet to freeze within thee.

Soft souls she binds in tender twist—
Small flies in spinner's web;
She sets afloat some luring streams,
But makes them soon to ebb.

Her watery eyes have burning force,
Her floods and flames conspire;
Tears kindle sparks, sobs fuel are,
And sighs do blow her fire.

May never was the month of Love,
For May is full of flowers;
But rather April, wet by kind,
For Love is full of showers.

Stanzas from Saint Peter's Complaint

(81)   WEEP balm and myrrh, you sweet Arabian trees,
       With purest gems perfume and pearl your rine;
    Shed on your honey drops, you busy bees.
    I, barren plant, must weep unpleasant brine.
    Hornets I hive, salt drops their labour plies
    Sucked out of sin and shed by show'ring eyes.

(96)   With easy loss sharp wrecks did he eschew
    That sindonless[1] aside did naked slip:
    Once naked Grace no outward garment knew;
    Rich are his robes, whom sin did never strip,
    I that in vaunts displayed Pride's fairest flags
    Disrobed of Grace, am wrapped in Adam's rags.

(121)   Sleep, death's ally, oblivion of tears,
    Silence of Passions, balm of angry sore,
    Suspense of loves, security of fears,
    Wrath's lenitive, heart's ease, storm's calmest shore,
    Sense's and soul's reprieval from all cumbers,
    Benumbing sense of ill with quiet slumbers.

(130)   Lazar at Pity's gate I ulcered lie
    Craving the refuse crumbs of children's plate;
    My sores I lay in view to Mercy's eye,
    My rags bear witness of my poor estate:
    The worms of Conscience that within me swarm,
    Prove that my plaints are less than is my harm.

[1] Shroudless.

ROBERT SOUTHWELL

Lewd Love is Loss

MISDEEMING eye! that stoopest to the lure
Of mortal worths, not worth so worthy love;
All beauty's base, all graces are impure
That do thy erring thoughts from God remove.
Sparks to the fire, the beams yield to the Sun,
All grace to God, from whom all graces run.

If picture more, more should the pattern please;
No shadow can with shadowed thing compare;
And fairest shapes, whereon our loves do cease,
But sely[1] signs of God's high beauties are.
Go, sterving sense, feed thou on earthly mast;
True love, in heaven seek thou thy sweet repast.

Glean not in barren soil these offal-ears,
Sith reap thou mayst whole heavens of delight;
Base joys with griefs, bad hopes do end in fears,
Lewd love with loss, evil peace with deadly fight:
God's love alone doth end with endless ease,
Whose joys in hope, whose hope concludes in peace.

Let not the luring train of fancies trap,
Or gracious features, proofs of Nature's skill,
Lull Reason's force asleep in Error's lap,
Or draw thy wit to bent of wanton will.
The fairest flowers have not the sweetest smell,
A seeming Heaven proves oft a damning Hell.

[1] Wondrous.

Self-pleasing souls that play with Beauty's bait
In shining shroud may swallow fatal hook;
Where eager sight on semblant fair doth wait
A lock it proves that first was but a look!
The fish with ease into the net doth glide,
But to get out the way is not so wide.

So long the fly doth dally with the flame
Until his singèd wings do force his fall;
So long the eye doth follow fancy's game
Till Love hath left the heart in heavy thrall.
Soon may the mind be cast in Cupid's gale,
But hard it is imprisoned thoughts to bail.

O loathe that Love whose final aim is lust,
Moth of the mind, eclipse of Reason's light;
The grave of Grace, the mole[1] of Nature's rust,
The wreck of Wit, the wrong of every Right.
In sum, an evil whose harms no tongue can tell;
In which to live is death, to die is Hell.

1 Fleshly mass.

ELIZABETHANS

JOHN BELLENDEN

(1533–1587)

A Starscape

WHEN silver Diane full of beames bright
    From dark eclipse was past, this other night
And in the Crab her proper mansion gain,
Artophilax contending at his might
In the great east to set his visage right,
I mean the leader of the Charlewain,
Above our head was the Urses twain;
When stars small obscuris in our sight
And Lu ifer left twinkling him alane.

(Proem to Boece.)

JOHN BELLENDEN

"*Anno Domini*"

WHEN golden Phoebus moved from the Ram
    Into the Bull to make his mansion,
And horned Diane in the Virgin came
With visage pale in her ascension,[1]
Approaching to her opposition;[1]
When dark Aurora with her misty showers
Fleeing of sky the bright reflexion,
Her silver tears scattered on the flowers.

The season when the great Octavian
Both earth and seas had in his governance
With diadem as roy Caesarian
In most excellent honour and pleasance
With every glore that might his fame advance,
Whom he the crown of high triumph had won,
By which Peace and royal ordinance
The furious Mars was blowing to the horn.[2]

The same time when God omnipotent
Beheld of men the great calamity,
And thought the time was then expedient
Man to redeem from thralled captivity,
And to reduce him to felicity
With body and soul to be glorificate
Which was condemned in the Limb[3] to lie
From he was first in sin prevaricate.

[1] Terms in astrology.   [2] Declared rebel.   [3] Limbo

WILLIAM BYRD

(1538–1623)

Songs

IN crystal towns and turrets richly set
  With glittering gems that shine against the sun
In regal rooms of jasper and of jet
Content of mind not always likes to won;[1]
But oftentimes it pleaseth her to stay
In simple cotes enclosed with walls of clay.

LET not the sluggish sleep
  Close up thy waking eye,
Until with judgement deep
Thy daily deeds thou try:
He that one sin in conscience keeps
When he to quiet goes,
More venturous is than he that sleeps
With twenty mortal foes.

[1] Dwell.

PHILIP MASSINGER

(1553–1640)

The Maid of Honour

(ACT V, SCENE II.)

FATHER PAULO:

LOOK on this Maid of Honour, now
   Truly honoured in her vow
She pays to heaven vain delight
By day, or pleasure of the night,
She no more thinks of this fair hair
(Favours for great kings to wear)
Must now be shorn; her rich array
Changed into a homely gray:
The dainties with which she was fed,
And her proud flesh pampered,
Must not be tasted; from the spring
For wine, cold water we will bring;
And with fasting mortify
The feasts of sensuality.
Her jewels, beads; and she must look
Not in a glass but holy book,
To teach her the ne'er erring way
To immortality.   O may
She as she purposes to be
A child new-born to piety
Persevere in it and good men
With saints and angels say Amen.

PHILIP MASSINGER

The Renegado

(ACT V, SCENE I)

VITELLI:

"**Y**ET there's one scruple with which I am much
Perplexed and troubled, which I know you can
Resolve me of."

JESUIT: "What is 't?"

VITELLI: "This, Sir, my bride.
Whom I first courted and then won, not with
Loose lays, poor flatteries, apish compliments,
But sacred and religious zeal, yet wants
The holy badge that should proclaim her fit
For these celestial nuptials: willing she is,
I know, to wear it as the choicest jewel,
On her fair forehead; but to you that well
Could do that work of grace, I know the Viceroy
Will never grant access. Now in a case
Of this necessity, I would gladly learn,
Whether in me, a layman without orders,
It may not be religious and lawful,
As we go to our deaths, to do that office?"

JESUIT:

"A Question in itself with much ease answered;
Midwives upon necessity perform it;
And knights that in the Holy Land fought for
The freedom of Jerusalem, when full
Of sweat and enemies' blood, have made their helmets
The fount, out of which with their holy hands
They drew that heavenly liquor; 'twas approved then
By the Holy Church, nor must I think it now,
In you, a work less pious."

185   G 2

PHILIP MASSINGER

Death Invoked

WHY art thou slow, thou rest of trouble, Death,
  To stop a wretch's breath
That calls on thee, and offers her sad heart
A prey unto thy dart?
I am not young nor fair; be therefore bold:
Sorrow hath made me old,
Deformed and wrinkled; all that I can crave
Is quiet in my grave.
Such as live happy, hold long life a jewel;
But to me thou art cruel
If thou end not my tedious misery,
And I soon cease to be.
Strike and strike home, then; pity unto me,
In one short hour's delay, is tyranny.

(From " The Emperor of the East.")

THOMAS LODGE

(1558–1625)

Phyllis

MY Phyllis hath the morning sun
    At first to look upon her;
And Phyllis hath morn-waking birds
    Her risings still to honour.
My Phyllis hath prime-feather'd flowers,
    That smile when she treads on them;
And Phyllis hath a gallant flock,
    That leaps since she doth own them
But Phyllis hath too hard a heart,
    Alas that she should have it !
It yields no mercy to desert,
    Nor grace to those that crave it

THOMAS LODGE

Love's Protestation

FIRST shall the heavens want starry light,
  The seas be robbed of their waves,
The day want sun, the sun want bright,
The night want shade, the dead men graves,
The April, flowers and leaf and tree,
Before I false my faith to thee.

First shall the tops of highest hills
By humble plains be overpried,
And poets scorn the Muses' quills,
And fish forsake the water-glide,
And Iris lose her coloured weed
Before I fail thee at thy need.

First direful hate shall turn to peace
And love relent in deep disdain,
And death his fatal stroke shall cease
And envy pity every pain,
And Pleasure mourn and Sorrow smile
Before I talk of any guile.

First Time shall stay his stayless race
And winter bless his boughs with corn,
And snow bemoisten July's face,
And winter spring and summer mourn
Before my pen, by help of Fame,
Cease to recite thy sacred name.

HENRY CONSTABLE

(1562–1613)

Love's Franciscan

SWEET hand ! the sweet yet cruel bow thou art,
From whence at one, five ivory arrows fly,
So with five wounds at once I wounded lie
Bearing in breast the print of every dart.
Saint Francis had the like, yet felt no smart:
Where I in living torments never die,
His wounds were in his hands and feet where I
All these same helpless wounds feel in my heart.
Now as Saint Francis (if a saint) am I.
The bow which shot these shafts a relic is;
I mean the hand, which is the reason why
So many for devotion thee would kiss,
And I thy glove kiss as a thing divine;
Thy arrows quiver, and thy relics shine.

HENRY CONSTABLE

To the Blessed Sacrament

WHEN Thee (O holy sacrificed Lamb)
  In severed signs I white and liquid see,
As in thy body slain I think on Thee,
Which pale by shedding of Thy blood became.
And when again I do behold the same
Veiled in white to be received of me,
Thou seemest in thy sindon[1] wrapt to be
Like to a corse, whose monument I am.
Buried in me, unto my soul appear,
Prison'd in earth, and banished from Thy sight,
Like our forefathers who in Limbo were,
Clear thou my thoughts, as thou didst give them light,
And as thou others freed from purging fire
Quench in my heart the flames of bad desire.

1 Shroud.

HENRY CONSTABLE

To Our Blessed Lady

IN that (O Queen of Queens) thy birth was free
From guilt, which others do of grace bereave,
When in their mothers' womb they life receive
God as his sole-borne daughter loved thee.
To match thee like thy birth's nobility,
He thee His Spirit for thy spouse did leave
Of whom thou didst His only Son conceive,
And so wast linked to all the Trinity.
Cease then, O Queens who earthly crowns do wear,
To glory in the pomp of worldly things;
If men such high respect unto you bear
Which daughters, wives, and mothers are of Kings,
What honour should unto that Queen be done
Who had your God for Father, Spouse and Son !

To Saint Margaret

FAIR Amazon of Heaven who tookst in hand
Saint Michael and Saint George to imitate,
And for a tyrant's love transformed to hate
Wast for thy lylly[1] faith retained in band,
Alone on foot and with thy naked hand
Thou didst like Michael and his host; and that
For which on horse armed George we celebrate
Whilst thou, like them, a dragon didst withstand.
Behold my soul shut in my body's gaol
The which the Drake[2] of Hell gapes to devour.
Teach me (o virgin) how thou didst prevail.
Virginity, thou sayest, was all thy aid:
Give me then purity instead of power,
And let my soul, made chaste, pass for a Maid.

[1] Loyal.   [2] Dragon.

HENRY CONSTABLE

To Saint Mary Magdalen

SWEET Saint, thou better canst declare to me
What pleasure is obtained by heavenly love,
Than they which other loves did never prove,
Or which in sex are differing from thee;
For like a woman-spouse my soul shall be,
Whom sinful passions once to lust did move
And since betrothed to God's Son above
Should be enamoured with His Deity.
My body is the garment of my spright
While as the daytime of my life doth last,
When death shall bring the night of my delight
My soul unclothed shall rest from labours past:
And claspéd in the arms of God enjoy
By sweet conjunction everlasting joy.

(Harl. MS. 7553.)

RICHARD VERSTEGAN (ROWLANDS)

(1565–1620)

Our Lady's Lullaby

UPON my lap my Sovereign sits,
  And sucks upon my breast;
Meanwhile, his love sustains my life,
And gives my body rest.

> *Sing lullaby, my little Boy.*
> *Sing lullaby, my life's Joy.*

When thou hast taken thy repast,
Repose, my Babe, on me;
So may thy Mother and thy Nurse
Thy cradle also be.

> *Sing lullaby.*

My Babe, my Bliss, my Child, my Choice,
My Fruit, my Flower, and Bud,
My Jesus, and my only Joy,
The Sum of all my good.

> *Sing lullaby.*

Thy fruit of death from Paradise
Made thee exiled mourn;
My Fruit of Life to Paradise
Makes joyful thy return.

> *Sing lullaby.*

RICHARD VERSTEGAN (ROWLANDS)

The shepherds left their keeping sheep
For joy to see my Lamb;
How may I more rejoice to see
Myself to be the Dam.
   Sing lullaby.

Three kings their treasure hither brought
Of incense, myrrh and gold,
The heaven's Treasure and the King
That here they might behold.
   Sing lullaby.

One sort an angel did direct;
A star did guide the other;
And all the fairest Son to see
That ever had a mother.

   Sing lullaby, my little Boy ;
   Sing lullaby, my life's Joy.

HENRY HAWKINS, Jesuit

(1571–1646)

The Bee

TO Bethlehem's silly shed, methinks I see
The Virgin hasten like a busy Bee;
Which in a tempest subject to be blown,
In lieu of ballast, bears a little stone;
As 'twere with oars beats to and fro his wings,
Collects heaven's dew, which to the hive he brings,
Within that store house lies the daily freight.
Lets fall the stone. Even so of greater weight,
Cut without hands the Virgin now is gone
To lay the prime and fundamental stone;
Heaven's dew condensed was in the honey-comb,
She was the Bee, the hive her sacred womb.

HENRY HAWKINS

Hoc Cygno Vinces[1]

WHEN mild Favonius breathes, with warbling throat
        The milk-white Swan chants with a sweeter note,
But sweeter yet her music far excels
When death approaches, which her tune foretells.
So th' Holy Spirit, breathing from above
Upon the Virgin, raised with wings of love
Her heavenly muse unto a higher strain
In her melodious Sonnet.   But again,
When gentle death drew near, she high aspires
To tune an anthem with the angel choirs.
Thy Cygnets (Mother Swan) on thee rely:
O make them white, that they may singing die!

1 A medieval play upon *Hoc signo vinces.*

SIR JOHN BEAUMONT

(1583-1627)

The Assumption

WHO is she that ascends so high,
　　Next the Heavenly King,
Round about whom Angels fly
　　And her praises sing?

Who is she that, adorned with light,
　　Makes the sun her robe,
At whose feet the queen of night
　　Lays her changing globe?

To that crown direct thine eye,
　　Which her head attires;
There thou mayst her name descry
　　Writ in starry fires.

This is she in whose pure womb
　　Heaven's Prince remained;
Therefore in no earthly tomb
　　Can she be contained.

Heaven she was, which held that fire,
　　Whence the world took light,
And to Heaven doth now aspire
　　Flames with flames t' unite.

She that did so clearly shine
　　When our day begun,
See how bright her beams decline
　　Now she sits with the Sun.

SIR JOHN BEAUMONT

On the Coincidence of the Feasts of the Annunciation and the Resurrection in 1627

THRICE happy day which sweetly dost combine
Two hemispheres in th' equinoctial line:
The one debasing God to earthly pain,
The other raising man to endless reign.
Christ's humble steps descending to the womb
Touch heavenly scales erected on his tomb.

FRANCIS BEAUMONT

(1584–1616)

On the Tombs in Westminster Abbey

MORTALITY, behold and fear!
What a change of flesh is here!
Think how many royal bones
Sleep within this heap of stones:
Here they lie had realms and lands,
Who now want strength to stir their hands:
Where from pulpits seal'd with dust
They preach, " In greatness is no trust."
Here's an acre sown indeed
With the richest, royall'st seed
That the earth did e'er suck in
Since the first man died for sin:
Here the bones of birth have cried—
" Though gods they were, as men they died."
Here are sands, ignoble things,
Dropt from the ruin'd sides of kings;
Here's a world of pomp and state,
Buried in dust, once dead by fate

JAMES SHIRLEY

(1596–1666)

Piping Peace

YOU virgins, that did late despair
  To keep your wealth from cruel men,
Tie up in silk your careless hair;
Soft peace is come again.

Now lovers' eyes may gently shoot
A flame that will not kill;
The drum was angry, but the lute
Shall whisper what you will.

Sing Io, Io ! for his sake
That hath restored your drooping heads;
With choice of sweetest flowers make
A garden where he treads;

Whilst we whole groves of laurel bring,
A petty triumph for his brow,
Who is the Master of our spring
And all the bloom we owe.

(From " The Imposture.")

201

JAMES SHIRLEY

The Passing Bell

HARK, how chimes the Passing bell,
There's no musick to a knell;
All the other sounds we hear,
Flatter, and but cheat our ear.

This doth put us still in mind
That our flesh must be resign'd,
And a general silence made,
The world be muffled in a shade;
He that on his pillow lies
Tear-enbalmed before he dies,
Carries like a sheep his life,
To meet the sacrificer's knife,
And for eternity is prest,
Sad Bell-wether to the rest.

JAMES SHIRLEY

A Song of Nuns

O FLY, my soul! What hangs upon
        Thy drooping wings
            And weighs them down
    With love of gaudy mortal things?

The sun is now the East; each shade
        As he doth rise
            Is shorter made
    That earth may lessen to our eyes.

O be but careless then, and play
        Until the Star of Peace
    Hide all his beams in dark recess.
    Poor pilgrims needs must lose their way
    When all the shadows do increase.

Bard's Chant

A MAN shall come into this land
        With shaven crown, and in his hand
    A crooked staff; he shall command
    And in the East his table stand:
    From his warm lips a stream shall flow
    To make rocks melt and churches grow.

(*From " Saint Patrick for Ireland."*

JAMES SHIRLEY

A Dirge

THE glories of our blood and state
  Are shadows, not substantial things;
There is no armour against Fate;
  Death lays his icy hand on kings:
     Sceptre and crown
     Must tumble down,
And in the dust be equal made
With the poor crooked scythe and spade.

Some men with swords may reap the field,
  And plant fresh laurels where they kill;
But their strong nerves at last must yield;
  They tame but one another still:
     Early or late
     They stoop to fate,
And must give up their murmuring breath,
When they, poor captives, creep to death.

The garlands wither on your brow,
  Then boast no more your mighty deeds !
Upon Death's purple altar now
  See, where the victor-victim bleeds:
     Your heads must come
     To the cold tomb,
Only the actions of the just
Smell sweet and blossom in the dust.

(From " Ajax and Ulysses.")

THE CAROLINES

SIR KENELM DIGBY

(1603–1665)

On His Late Espoused Saint

BURIED in the shades of horrid night
  My vexed soul doth groan, exiled from light;
And ghastly dreams
Are now the themes
That my frighted fancy feeds itself withal.

And to add afflictions with new pain
Despairing thoughts possess my restless brain,
Persuading me
That I ne'er shall see
Her that only can my past blest hours recall.

Like to the pale planet that doth reign
Queen of the darkness, if the dusky train
Of th' earth's black robe
Reach up to her globe,
All the light and beauty that she had is gone.

WILLIAM HABINGTON

(1605–1654)

" *Nox nocti indicat scientiam* "

WHEN I survey the bright
 Celestial sphere;
So rich with jewels hung, that night
 Doth like an Ethiop bride appear:

My soul her wings doth spread
 And heavenward flies,
The Almighty's mysteries to read
 In the large volumes of the skies.

For the bright firmament
 Shoots forth no flame
So silent, but is eloquent
 In speaking the Creator's name.

No unregarded star
 Contracts its light
Into so small a character
 Removed far from our human sight,

But if we steadfast look
 We shall discern
In it, as in some holy book,
 How man may heavenly knowledge learn.

It tells the conqueror
 That far-stretched power,
Which his proud dangers traffic for,
 Is but the triumph of an hour;

That from the farthest North,
  Some nation may,
Yet undiscovered, issue forth,
  And o'er his new-got conquest sway

Some nation yet shut in
  With hills of ice
May be let out to scourge his sin,
  Till they shall equal him in vice.

And then they likewise shall
  Their ruin have;
For as yourselves your empires fall,
  And every kingdom hath a grave.

Thus those celestial fires,
  Though seeming mute,
The fallacy of our desires
  And all the pride of life confute:

For they have watched since first
  The world had birth;
And found sin in itself accursed,
  And nothing permanent on earth.

WILLIAM HABINGTON

" *Recogitabo tibi omnes annos meos* "

TIME! where didst thou those years intei
    Which I have seen decease?
My soul's at war and Truth bids her
Find out their hidden Sepulchre
    To give her troubles peace.

Pregnant with flowers doth not the Spring
    Like a late Bride appear?
Whose feathered music only bring
Caresses and no Requiem sing
    On the departed year.

The Earth like some rich wanton heir
    Whose parents coffined lie,
Forgets it once looked pale and bare
And doth for vanities prepare
    As the Spring ne'er should die.

WILLIAM HABINGTON

" *Quoniam ego in flagella paratus sum* "

ETERNITY, when I think thee
(Which never any end must have
Nor knewest beginning) and foresee
Hell is designed for sin a grave.

My frighted flesh trembles to dust,
My blood ebbs fearfully away:
Both guilty that they did to lust
And vanity my youth betray.

My eyes which from each beauteous sight
Drew spider-like black venom in,
Close like the Marigold at night,
Oppressed with dew to bathe my sin.

My ears shut up that easy door
Which did proud fallacies admit,
And vow to hear no follies more,
Deaf to the charms of sin and wit.

My hands (which when they touched some fair
Imagined such an excellence
As th' Ermine's skin ungentle were)
Contract themselves and loose all sense.

No sorrow then shall enter in
With pity the great Judge's ears.
This moment's ours. Once dead, his sin
Men cannot expiate with tears.

WILLIAM HABINGTON

The Reward of Innocent Love

WE saw and woo'd each other's eyes,
  My soul contracted then with thine,
And both burnt in one sacrifice
By which our marriage grew divine.

Let wilder youths, whose soul is sense,
Profane the temple of delight,
And purchase endless penitence
With the stolen pleasure of one night.

Time 's ever ours, while we despise
The sensual idol of our clay,
For though the sun do set and rise
We joy one everlasting day.

Whose light no jealous clouds obscure,
While each of us shine innocent.
The troubled stream is still impure:
With virtue flies away content.

And though opinion often err,
We'll court the modest smile of fame,
For sin's black danger circles her
Who hath infection in her name.

Thus when to one dark silent room
Death shall our loving coffins thrust,
Fame will build columns on our tomb,
And add a perfume to our dust.

WILLIAM HABINGTON

Upon Thought Castara may Die

IF she should die (as well suspect we may,
A body so compact should ne'er decay)
Her brighter soul would in the Moon inspire
More chastity, in dimmer stars more fire.
You twins of Leda (as your parents are
In their wild lusts) may grow irregular
Now in your motion: for the Mariner
Henceforth shall only steer his course by her.
And when the zeal of aftertimes shall spy
Her uncorrupt i' th' happy marble lie;
The roses in her cheeks unwithered,
'Twill turn to love and dote upon the dead.
For he who did to her in life dispense
A Heaven, will banish all corruption thence.

The Compliment

CUPID did cry, his mother chid him so,
And all because the child had lost his bow.
But how! with no intent that she should have it
He met my Mistress and to her he gave it,
Excusing it: one was so like the other
That he mistook and took her for his mother.

(*From MS.*)

SIR WILLIAM DAVENANT

(1606–1668)

Morning

THE lark now leaves his watery nest,
    And climbing shakes his dewy wings,
He takes your window for the east,
    And to implore your light, he sings;
Awake, awake, the morn will never rise,
Till she can dress her beauty at your eyes.

The merchant bows unto the seaman's star,
    The ploughman from the sun his season takes;
But still the lover wonders what they are,
    Who look for day before his mistress wakes;
Awake, awake, break through your veils of lawn!
Then draw your curtains and begin the dawn.

SIR WILLIAM DAVENANT

Lover and Philosopher

LOVER:

" YOUR beauty ripe and calm and fresh
As eastern summers are,
Must now forsaking Time and Flesh
Add light to some small star."

PHILOSOPHER:

" While she yet lives, were stars decayed,
Their light by hers relief might find.
But Death will lead her to a shade
Where Love is cold and Beauty blind."

LOVER:

" Lovers (whose Priests all Poets are)
Think any mistress when she dies
Is changed at least into a star,
And who dares doubt the Poet's wise ?"

PHILOSOPHER:

" But ask not bodies doomed to die
To what abode they go;
Since Knowledge is but Sorrow's Spy,
It is not safe to know."

SIR WILLIAM DAVENANT

Epitaph

WHEN you perceive these stones are wet
Think not you see the Marble sweat;
It weeps for grief the Day of Doom
(Invoked by Saints) will shortly come;
Then the unwilling Marble must
Surrender all this Saint's sweet dust.

RICHARD CRASHAW

(1613–1649)

"*Quaerit Jesum suum Maria*"

AND is he gone, whom these arms held but now
  Their hope, their vow?
Did ever grief and joy in one poor heart
  So soon change part?
He's gone; the fair'st flower that e'er bosom dress'd,
  My soul's sweet rest.
My womb's chaste pride is gone, my heaven-born boy:
  And where is joy?
He's gone; and his lov'd steps to wait upon,
  My joy is gone.
My joys and he are gone, my grief and I
  Alone must lie.
He's gone; not leaving with me, till he come,
  One smile at home.
Oh, come then, bring Thy mother her lost joy:
  Oh come, sweet boy.
Make haste and come, or e'er my grief and I
  Make haste and die.
Peace, heart! the heavens are angry, all their spheres
  Rival thy tears.
I was mistaken, some fair sphere or other
  Was thy blest mother.
What but the fairest heaven could own the birth
  Of so fair earth?
Yet sure thou didst lodge here; this womb of mine
  Was once call'd thine.
Oft have these arms thy cradle envièd,
  Beguil'd thy bed.

Oft to thy easy ears hath this shrill tongue
    Trembled and sung.
Oft have I wrapped thy slumbers in soft airs,
    And strok'd thy cares.
Oft hath this hand those silken casements kept,
    While their suns slept.
Oft have my hungry kisses made thine eyes
    Too early rise.
Oft have I spoil'd my kisses' daintiest diet,
    To spare thy quiet.
Oft from this breast to thine my love-toss'd heart
    Hath leapt, to part.
Oft my lost soul have I been glad to seek
    On thy soft cheek.
Oft have these arms, alas, show'd to these eyes
    Their now lost joys.
Dawn then to me, thou morn of mine own day,
    And let heaven stay.
Oh, would'st thou here still fix thy fair abode,
    My bosom God:
What hinders but my bosom still might be
    Thy heaven to Thee?

RICHARD CRASHAW

Hymn to Saint Teresa

LOVE, thou art absolute, sole Lord
Of life and death. To prove the word,
We'll now appeal to none of all
Those thy old soldiers, great and tall,
Ripe men of martyrdom, that could reach down
With strong arms their triumphant crown;
Such as could with lusty breath
Speak loud into the face of Death,
Their great Lord's glorious name, to none
Of those whose spacious bosoms spread a throne
For Love at large to fill; spare blood and sweat
And see Him take a private seat,
And make His mansion in the mild
And milky soul of a soft child.

    Scarce has she learnt to lisp the name
Of martyr; yet she thinks it shame
Life should so long play with that breath
Which spent can buy so brave a death.
She never undertook to know
What Death with Love should have to do;
Nor has she e'er yet understood
Why to show love she should shed blood,
Yet tho' she cannot tell you why,
She can love, and she can die.

    Scarce has she blood enough to make
A guilty sword blush for her sake;
Yet has a heart dares hope to prove
How much less strong is Death than Love.

    Be Love but there; let poor six years
Be posed with the maturest fears

Man trembles at, you straight shall find
Love knows no nonage, nor the mind;
'Tis love, not years or limbs that can
Make the martyr, or the man.

Love touched her heart, and lo it beats
High, and burns with such brave heats;
Such thirsts to die, as dares drink up
A thousand cold deaths in one cup.
Good reason, for she breathes all fire;
Her white breast heaves with strong desire
Of what she may, with fruitless wishes,
Seek for amongst her mother's kisses.

Since 'tis not to be had at home
She'll travel to a martyrdom.
No home for hers confesses she
But where she may a martyr be.

She'll to the Moors; and trade with them
For this unvalued diadem;
She'll offer them her dearest breath,
With Christ's name in 't, in change for death:
She'll bargain with them, and will give
Them God; and teach them how to live
In Him: or, if they this deny,
For Him she'll teach them how to die.
So shall she leave amongst them sown
Her Lord's blood; or at least her own.

Farewell then, all the world adieu!
Teresa is no more for you.
Farewell, all pleasures, sports, and joys
(Never till now esteemèd toys),
Farewell, whatever dear may be,
Mother's arms, or father's knee:

RICHARD CRASHAW

Farewell house, and farewell home !
She's for the Moors, and martyrdom.
   Sweet, not so fast ! lo, thy fair Spouse,
Whom thou seek'st with so swift vows,
Calls thee back, and bids thee come
T' embrace a milder martyrdom. . . .
   O how oft shalt thou complain
Of a sweet and subtle pain:
Of intolerable joys;
Of a death, in which who dies
Loves his death, and dies again,
And would for ever so be slain.
And lives and dies; and knows not why
To live; but that he thus may never leave to die
   How kindly will thy gentle heart
Kiss the sweetly-killing dart,
And close in his embraces keep
Those delicious wounds, that weep
Balsam to heal themselves with; thus,
When these thy deaths, so numerous,
Shall all at last die into one,
And melt thy soul's sweet mansion;
Like a soft lump of incense, hasted
By too hot a fire, and wasted
Into perfuming clouds, so fast
Shalt thou exhale to heaven at last
In a resolving sigh, and then
O what ? Ask not the tongues of men;
Angels cannot tell; suffice
Thyself shalt feel thine own full joys,
And hold them fast for ever there,
So soon as thou shalt first appear,

The moon of maiden stars, thy white
Mistress, attended by such bright
Souls as thy shining self shall come,
And in her first ranks make thee room;
Where 'mongst her snowy family
Immortals' welcomes wait for thee.

O what delight, when revealed Life shall stand
And teach thy lips Heaven, with His hand;
On which thou now may'st to thy wishes
Heap up thy consecrated kisses !
What joy shall seize thy soul when she,
Bending her blessèd eyes on thee,
Those second smiles of Heaven, shall dart
Her mild rays through thy melting heart !

Angels, thy old friends, there shall greet thee,
Glad at their own home now to meet thee.
All thy good works which went before
And waited for thee at the door,
Shall own thee there; and all in one
Weave a constellation
Of crowns, with which the King, thy Spouse,
Shall build up thy triumphant brows.
All thy old woes shall now smile on thee,
And thy pains sit bright upon thee,
All thy sorrows here shall shine,
And thy sufferings be divine:
Tears shall take comfort, and turn gems,
And wrongs repent to diadems.
Even thy deaths shall live, and new
Dress the soul which late they slew.
Thy wounds shall blush to such bright scars
As keep account of the Lamb's wars.

Those rare works, where thou shalt leave writ
Love's noble history, with wit
Taught thee by none but Him, while here
They feed our souls, shall clothe thine there.
Each heavenly word by whose hid flame
Our hard hearts shall strike fire, the same
Shall flourish on thy brows, and be
Both fire to us and flame to thee;
Whose light shall live bright in thy face
By glory, in our hearts by grace.
    Thou shalt look round about, and see
Thousands of crown'd souls throng to be
Themselves thy crown: sons of thy vows,
The virgin-births with which thy sovereign Spouse
Made fruitful thy fair soul.   Go now
And with them all about thee, bow
To Him; put on, He'll say, put on,
My rosy Love, that thy rich zone,
Sparkling with the sacred flames
Of thousand souls, whose happy names
Heaven keeps upon thy score: thy bright
Life brought them first to kiss the light
That kindled them to stars, and so
Thou with the Lamb, thy Lord, shalt go,
And wheresoe'er He sets His white
Steps, walk with Him those ways of light,
Which who in death would live to see,
Must learn in life to die like thee.

RICHARD CRASHAW

The Shepherds' Hymn

WE saw Thee in Thy balmy nest,
  Young dawn of our eternal Day;
We saw Thine eyes break from their East,
  And chase the trembling shades away:
We saw Thee: and we blessed the sight,
We saw Thee by Thine own sweet light.

Poor world, said I, what wilt thou do
  To entertain this starry Stranger ?
Is this the best thou canst bestow—
  A cold and not too cleanly manger ?
Contend, the powers of Heaven and Earth,
To fit a bed for this huge birth.

Proud world, said I, cease your contest,
  And let the mighty babe alone;
The phœnix builds the phœnix' nest,
  Love's architecture is his own.
The babe whose birth embraves this morn,
Made His own bed ere He was born.

I saw the curl'd drops, soft and slow,
  Come hovering o'er the place's head;
Offering their whitest sheets of snow,
  To furnish the fair infant's bed.
Forbear, said I, be not too bold;
Your fleece is white, but 'tis too cold.

RICHARD CRASHAW

I saw th' obsequious Seraphim
   Their rosy fleece of fire bestow,
For well they now can spare their wing,
   Since Heaven itself lies here below.
Well done, said I; but are you sure
Your down, so warm, will pass for pure?

No, no! your King's not yet to seek
   Where to repose His royal head;
See, see, how soon His new-bloom'd cheek
   'Twixt mother's breasts is gone to bed!
Sweet choice, said we! no way but so,
Not to lie cold, yet sleep in snow.

She sings thy tears asleep, and dips
   Her kisses in Thy weeping eye;
She spreads the red leaves of Thy lips,
   That in their buds yet blushing lie.
She 'gainst those mother diamonds tries
The points of her young eagle's eyes.

Welcome, all wonders in one sight!
   Eternity shut in a span!
Summer in Winter, Day in Night!
   Heaven in Earth, and God in Man!
Great little One! whose all-embracing birth
Lifts Earth to Heaven, stoops Heaven to Earth.

Welcome, tho' not to gold nor silk,
   To more than Cæsar's birthright is;
Two sister-seas of Virgin-milk,
   With many a rarely temper'd kiss,
That breathes at once both maid and mother,
Warms in the one, cools in the other.

225

RICHARD CRASHAW

Welcome, tho' not to those gay flies,
  Gilded i' the beams of earthly kings;
Slippery souls in shining eyes,
  But to poor shepherds, homespun things,
Whose wealth's their flocks, whose wit's to be
Well-read in their simplicity.

Yet, when young April's husband-showers
  Shall bless the fruitful Maia's bed,
We'll bring the first-born of her flowers
  To kiss Thy feet, and crown Thy head;
To Thee, dread Lamb ! whose love must keep
The shepherds more than they keep sheep.

To Thee, meek Majesty ! soft King
  Of simple graces and sweet Loves:
Each of us his lamb will bring,
  Each his pair of silver doves:
Till burnt at last in fire of Thy fair eyes,
Ourselves become our own best sacrifice !

EPIGRAMS

(1) *To Our Blessed Lord upon the Choice of His Sepulchre*

HOW life and death in Thee
    Agree !
Thou hadst a virgin womb,
    And tomb.
A Joseph did betroth
    Them both.

(2) *Upon the Body of Our Blessed Lord Naked and Bloody*

THEY have left Thee naked, Lord; O that they had
  This garment too I would they had denied.
Thee with Thyself they have too richly clad
Opening the purple wardrobe of Thy side.
O never could there be garment too good
For Thee to wear but this of Thine own blood.

(3) *On the Miracle of Loaves*

NOW Lord or never they'll believe on Thee;
  Thou to their teeth hast proved Thy Deity.

(4) *On Dives*

A DROP, one drop, how sweetly one fair drop
Would tremble on my pearl-tipped finger's top ?
My wealth is gone, O go it where it will.
Spare this one Jewel; I'll be Dives still !

(5) *" Qui perdiderit animam suam "*

S O I may gain thy death, my life I'll give;
My life's thy death and in thy death I live;
Or else, my life, I'll hide thee in his grave,
By three days' loss eternally to save.

(6) *St Peter's Shadow*

U NDER thy shadow may I lurk awhile,
Death's busy search I'll easily beguile;
Thy shadow, Peter, must show me the Sun,
My light's thy shadow's shadow, or 'tis done.

RICHARD FLECKNOE, Priest

(1575–1678)

Noble Love

IT is the counterpoise that minds
　To fair and virtuous things inclines;
It is the gust we have and sense
Of every noble excellence;
It is the pulse by which we know
Whether our souls have life or no;
And such a soft and gentle fire
As kindles and inflames desire;
Until it all like incense burns
And unto melting sweetness turns.

SIR EDWARD SHERBURNE

(1618–1702)

" *Christus Mathaeum et Discipulos Alloquitur* "

L EAVE, leave, converted publican ! lay down
    That sinful trash, which in thy happier race,
To gain a heavenly crown,
Clogs thy free pace.
O ! what for this pale dirt will not man do ?
Nay, even now, 'mongst you
(For this) there's one I see,
Seeks to sell me.
But times will come hereafter, when for gold
I shall by more (alas !) than one be sold.

SIR EDWARD SHERBURNE

The Magdalen

THE proud Egyptian queen, her Roman guest,
  (T' express her love in height of state and pleasure)
With pearl dissolv'd in gold, did feast,
  Both food and treasure.

And no v (dear Lord !) thy lover, on the fair
  And silver tables of Thy feet, behold !
Pearl, in her tears and in her hair,
  Offers thee gold.

SIR EDWARD SHERBURNE

Conscience

INTERNAL Cerberus, whose griping fangs
That gnaw the soul are the Mind's secret pangs,
Thou greedy Vulture that dost gorging tire
On hearts corrupted by impure desire.
Subtle and buzzing Hornet ! that dost ring
A peal of horror ere thou givest the sting.
The soul's rough file that smoothness does impart,
The hammer that does break a stony heart,
The worm that never dies ! the thorn within
That pricks and pains: the whip and scourge of sin;
The voice of God in Man ! which without rest
Doth softly cry within a troubled Breast;
To all temptations is that soul left free
That makes not to itself a curb of me.

WILLIAM WYCHERLY

(1640–1716)

To a Good Physician

BUT you can Life upon the Poor bestow,
　　Without return like Life's First Giver too;
Nay, like the Great Physician of the Soul,
Do good against our Wills, our Fates control;
In your self you, what is most hard to do,
By those, whom of your Faculty, we know,
All evils cure of your Profession too;
Pride's Tympany,[1] Hydropic[2] Avarice
Against which, few can give themselves Advice;
Unlike them, you make Patients ne'er endure,
Less Danger, Pain, from their Disease than Cure;
We both serve the same Saving Deity,
The God of Physic and of Poetry,
By which men think to live immortally;
Could I prevent your death, as mine you do,
You then should live by me, as I by you; .
Which, if by any's Art, it could be done,
Could be, by none sure, so sure as your own;
You make Fate on you not on it wait,
Thus overpowering it, you grow Fate's Fate;
Not, like your Brethren, its Minister,
Fate's King and not its Executioner.

[1] Dropsical.　　　　　[2] Blister.

THE CLASSICAL

JOHN DRYDEN

(1631–1700)

The Churches of Rome and of England

A MILK-WHITE Hind, immortal and unchanged,
Fed on the lawns, and in the forest ranged;
Without unspotted, innocent within,
She feared no danger, for she knew no sin.
Yet had she oft been chased with horns and hounds
And Scythian shafts, and many wingèd wounds
Aimed at her heart; was often forced to fly
And doomed to death, though fated not to die.

Not so her young; for their unequal line
Was Hero's make, half human, half divine:
Their early mould obnoxious was to fate,
Th' immortal part assumed immortal state.
Of these a slaughtered army lay in blood,
Extended o'er the Caledonian wood,
Their native walk; whose vocal blood arose,
And cried for pardon on their perjured foes.
Their fate was fruitful, and the sanguine seed
Endued with souls, increased the sacred breed.
So captive Israel multiplied in chains,
A numerous exile, and enjoyed her pains.
With grief and gladness mixed, the mother viewed
Her martyred offspring, and their race renewed;
Their corpse to perish, but their kind to last,
So much the deathless plant the dying fruit surpassed.

Panting and pensive now she ranged alone,
And wandered in the kingdoms once her own.
The common hunt though from their rage restrained
By sovereign power, her company disdained,

Grinned as they passed, and with a glaring eye
Gave gloomy sighs of secret enmity.
'Tis true she bounded by, and tripped so light,
They had not time to take a steady sight:
For truth has such a face and such a mien,
As to be loved needs only to be seen. . . .

The Panther, sure the noblest next the Hind,
And fairest creature of the spotted kind;
Oh, could her inborn stains be washed away,
She were too good to be a beast of prey !
How can I praise or blame, and not offend,
Or how divide the frailty from the friend ?
Her faults and virtues lie so mixed, that she
Nor wholly stands condemned nor wholly free.
Then like her injured Lion let me speak;
He cannot bend her, and he would not break.
Unkind already, and estranged in part,
The Wolf begins to share her wandering heart;
Though unpolluted yet with actual ill,
The half commits who sins but in her will.
If, as our dreaming Platonists report,
There could be spirits of a middle sort,
Too black for heaven, yet too white for hell,
Who just dropped half-way down, nor lower fell,
So poised, so gently she descends from high,
It seems a soft dismission from the sky.
Her house not ancient, whatsoe'er pretence
Her clergy heralds make in her defence;
A second century not half-way run,
Since the new honours of her blood begun.
A Lion[1] old, obscene, and furious made

[1] Henry VIII.

By lust, compressed her mother in a shade.
Then by a left-hand marriage weds the dame,
Covering adultery with a specious name:
So Schism begot; and Sacrilege and she,
A well-match'd pair, got graceless Heresy.
God's and king's rebels have the same good cause
To trample down divine and human laws:
Both would be called reformers, and their hate,
Alike destructive both to Church and State,
The fruit proclaims the plant; a lawless prince
By luxury reformed incontinence;
By ruins, charity; by riots, abstinence.
Confessions, fasts, and penance set aside;
Oh, with what ease we follow such a guide,
Where souls are starved, and senses gratified !
Where marriage pleasures mid-night prayer supply,
And matin bells, a melancholy cry,
Are tuned to merrier notes, increase and multiply.
Religion shows a rosy-coloured face,
Not battered out with drudging works of grace:
A downhill reformation rolls apace.
What flesh and blood would crowd the narrow gate,
Or, till they waste their pampered paunches, wait ?
All would be happy at the cheaper rate.

(From " The Hind and the Panther.")

JOHN DRYDEN

The Church's Testimony

BUT, gracious God ! how well dost Thou provide
　For erring judgments an unerring guide !
Thy throne is darkness in the abyss of light,
A blaze of glory that forbids the sight.
O teach me to believe Thee thus concealed,
And search no further than Thy self revealed;
But her alone for my director take
Whom Thou hast promised never to forsake !
My thoughtless youth was winged with vain desires,
My manhood, long misled by wandering fires,
Followed false lights; and when their glimpse was gone
My pride struck out new sparkles of her own.
Such was I, such by nature still I am;
Be Thine the glory, and be mine the shame !

(From " The Hind and the Panther.")

JOHN DRYDEN

The Popish Plot

THE inhabitants of old Jerusalem[1]
    Were Jebusites,[2] the town so called from them;
And theirs the native right—
But when the chosen people grew more strong,
The rightful cause at length became the wrong;
And every loss the men of Jebus bore,
They still were thought God's enemies the more.
Thus worn or weakened, well or ill content,
Submit they must to David's[3] government:
Impoverished and deprived of all command,
Their taxes doubled as they lost their land;
And what was harder yet to flesh and blood,
Their Gods disgraced, and burned like common wood. . .
. . . From hence began the Plot, the nation's curse
Bad in itself, but represented worse;
Raised in extremes, and in extremes decried;
With oaths affirmed, with dying vows denied;
Not weighed nor winnowed by the multitude;
But swallowed in the mass, unchewed and crude.
Some truth there was, but dashed and brewed with lies,
To please the fools and puzzle all the wise,
Succeeding times did equal folly call,
Believing nothing or believing all.

(*From "Absolom and Achitophel."*)

[1] London.   [2] Catholics.   [3] Charles II.

JOHN DRYDEN

Alexander's Feast

(An Ode in Honour of St Cecilia's Day, 1697)

'TWAS at the royal feast, for Persia won,
    By Philip's warlike son—
Aloft in awful state
The godlike hero sate
    On his imperial throne;
His valiant peers were placed around,
Their brows with roses and with myrtles bound:
    (So should desert in arms be crowned);
The lovely Thais by his side
Sate like a blooming Eastern bride,
In flower of youth and beauty's pride.
        Happy, happy, happy pair !
        None but the brave,
        None but the brave,
        None but the brave deserves the fair !

Timotheus, placed on high
    Amid the tuneful quire,
    With flying fingers touch'd the lyre:
The trembling notes ascend the sky,
    And heavenly joys inspire.
The song began from Jove,
Who left his blissful seats above—
Such is the power of mighty love !
A dragon's fiery form belied the god;
Sublime on radiant spires he rode,
        When he to fair Olympia pressed,
        And while he sought her snowy breast;

Then round her slender waist he curl'd,
And stamp'd an image of himself, a sovereign of the world
The listening crowd admire the lofty sound !
A present deity ! they shout around:
A present deity ! the vaulted roofs rebound:
With ravish'd ears
The monarch hears,
Assumes the god;
Affects to nod,
And seems to shake the spheres.

The praise of Bacchus then the sweet musician sung:
Of Bacchus ever fair and ever young:
The jolly god in triumph comes !
Sound the trumpet, beat the drums !
Flush'd with a purple grace
He shows his honest face:
Now give the hautboys breath; he comes, he comes !
Bacchus ever fair and young,
Drinking joys did first ordain;
Bacchus' blessings are a treasure,
Drinking is the soldier's pleasure:
Rich the treasure,
Sweet the pleasure,
Sweet is pleasure after pain.

Sooth'd with the sound the king grew vain;
Fought all his battles o'er again;
And thrice he routed all his foes, and thrice he slew the slain
The master saw the madness rise;
His glowing cheeks, his ardent eyes;

And while he heaven and earth defied,
Changed his hand and check'd his pride.
   He chose a mournful muse
   Soft pity to infuse:
He sung Darius great and good,
  By too severe a fate
Fallen, fallen, fallen, fallen,
Fallen from his high estate,
 And weltering in his blood;
Deserted, at his utmost need,
By those his former bounty fed;
On the bare earth exposed he lies,
With not a friend to close his eyes.
With downcast looks the joyless victor sate,
 Revolving in his alter'd soul
  The various turns of Chance below;
And now and then a sigh he stole,
  And tears began to flow.

  The mighty master smil'd to see
  That love was in the next degree;
'Twas but a kindred sound to move,
For pity melts the mind to love.
Softly sweet, in Lydian measures,
Soon he sooth'd his soul to pleasures
War, he sung, is toil and trouble,
Honour but an empty bubble;
 Never ending, still beginning,
Fighting still, and still destroying;
 If the world be worth thy winning,
Think, oh think it worth enjoying;

JOHN DRYDEN

Lovely Thais sits beside thee,
Take the goods the gods provide thee!
The many rend the skies with loud applause;
So Love was crowned, but Music won the cause.
The prince, unable to conceal his pain,
Gazed on the fair
Who caused his care,
And sigh'd and look'd, sigh'd and look'd,
Sigh'd and look'd, and sigh'd again:
At length, with love and wine at once oppressed,
The vanquished victor sunk upon her breast.

Now strike the golden lyre again:
A louder yet, and yet a louder strain!
Break his bands of sleep asunder,
And rouse him, like a rattling peal of thunder.
Hark, hark! the horrid sound
Has raised up his head:
As awaked from the dead,
And amazed he stares around.
Revenge, revenge, Timotheus cries,
See the furies arise!
See the snakes that they rear,
How they hiss in their hair,
And the sparkles that flash from their eyes!
Behold a ghastly band,
Each a torch in his hand!
Those are Grecian ghosts, that in battle were slain,
And unburied remain
Inglorious on the plain:
Give the vengeance due
To the valiant crew!

JOHN DRYDEN

Behold how they toss their torches on high,
  How they point to the Persian abodes,
  And glittering temples of their hostile gods.
The princes applaud with a furious joy;
And the king seized a flambeau with zeal to destroy;
        This led the way,
        To light him his prey,
And like another Helen, fired another Troy !

        Thus, long ago,
        Ere heaving billows learn'd to blow,
        While organs yet were mute,
        Timotheus, to his breathing flute
        And sounding lyre
Could swell the soul to rage, or kindle soft desire.
        At last divine Cecilia came,
        Inventress of the vocal frame;
The sweet enthusiast, from her sacred store,
        Enlarged the former narrow bounds,
        And added length to solemn sounds,
With Nature's mother-wit, and arts unknown before.
        Let old Timotheus yield the prize,
        Or both divide the crown;
        He raised a mortal to the skies;
        She drew an angel down !

Upon the Death of the Earl of Dundee

O LAST and best of Scots! who didst maintain
　Thy country's freedom from a foreign reign;
New people fill the land now thou art gone,
New gods the temples and new kings the throne.
Scotland and thee did each in other live
Nor wouldst thou her, nor could she thee survive.
Farewell, who dying didst support the state
And couldst not fall but with thy country's fate.

King James II

S LOW to resolve, but in performance quick;
　So true, that he was awkward at a trick.
For little souls on little shifts rely,
And coward arts of mean expedients try:
The noble mind will dare do anything but lie.
False friends (his deadliest foes) could find no way
But shows of honest bluntness, to betray;
That unsuspected plainness he believed;
He looked into himself, and was deceived.

(From " The Hind and the Panther.")

JOHN DRYDEN

The Portrait of Milton

THREE poets, in three distant ages born,
Greece, Italy and England did adorn.
The first in loftiness of thought surpassed,
The next in majesty, in both the last,
The force of Nature could no further go;
To make a third she joined the former two.

Midnight

ALL things are hushed, as Nature's self lay dead;
The mountains seem to nod their drowsy head,
The little birds in dreams their songs repeat,
And sleeping flowers beneath the night-dew sweat;
Even lust and envy sleep, yet love denies
Rest to my soul and slumber to my eyes.

JOHN DRYDEN

Conversion

BE vengeance wholly left to powers divine,
  And let Heaven judge betwixt your sons and mine:
If joys hereafter must be purchased here
With loss of all that mortals hold so dear,
Then welcome infamy and public shame,
And, last, a long farewell to worldly fame.
'Tis said with ease, but oh, how hardly tried
By haughty souls to human honour tied !
O sharp convulsive pangs of agonizing pride !
Down then, thou rebel, never more to rise;
And what thou didst and dost so dearly prize,
That fame, that darling fame, make that thy sacrifice.
'Tis nothing thou hast given; then add thy tears
For a long race of unrepenting years:
'Tis nothing yet; yet all thou hast to give:
Then add those may-be years thou hast to live.
Yet nothing still: then poor and naked come,
Thy Father will receive his unthrift home,
And thy blest Saviour's blood discharge the mighty sum

(*From " The Hind and the Panther."*)

JOHN DRYDEN

Love's Despair

FAREWELL, ungrateful traitor,
Farewell, my perjured swain !
Let never injured creature
Believe a man again.
The pleasure of possessing
Surpasses all expressing;
But 'tis too short a blessing
And love too long a pain.

'Tis easy to deceive us
In pity of your pain;
But when we love, you leave us
To rail at you in vain.
Before we have decried it,
There is no bliss beside it;
But she that once has tried it
Will never love again.

The passion you pretended
Was only to obtain,
But when the charm is ended
The charmer you disdain.
Your love by ours we measure,
Till we have lost our treasure;
But dying is a pleasure
When living is a pain.

(*From " The Spanish Friar."*)

ALEXANDER POPE

(1688–1744)

The Vestal

HOW happy is the blameless vestal's lot !
     The world forgetting, by the world forgot :
Eternal sunshine of the spotless mind !
Each prayer accepted, and each wish resign'd,
Labour and rest that equal periods keep:
" Obedient slumbers that can wake and weep ";
Desires composed, affections ever even;
Tears that delight, and sighs that waft to Heaven
Grace shines around her with serenest beams,
And whisp'ring angels prompt her golden dreams;
For her th' unfading rose of Eden blooms,
And wings of seraphs shed divine perfumes;
For her the spouse prepares the bridal ring,
For her white virgins hymeneals sing;
To sounds of heavenly harps she dies away,
And melts in visions of eternal day.

(From " Eloise and Abelar ")*

ALEXANDER POPE

Elegy to the Memory of an Unfortunate Lady

O EVER beauteous, ever friendly, tell,
  Is it, in Heaven, a crime to love too well —
To bear too tender or too firm a heart,
To act a lover's or a Roman's part ?
Is there no bright reversion in the sky
For those who greatly think, or bravely die ?
Why bade be else, ye Powers, her soul aspire
Above the vulgar flight of low desire ?
Ambition first sprung from your blest abodes—
The glorious fault of angels and of gods;
Thence to their images on earth it flows,
And in the breasts of kings and heroes glows.
Most souls, 'tis true, but peep out once an age,
Dull sullen prisoners in the body's cage:
Dim lights of life, that burn a length of years,
Useless, unseen, as lamps in sepulchres;
Like Eastern kings a lazy state they keep,
And, close confined to their own palace, sleep.
From these perhaps (ere Nature bade her die)
Fate snatched her early to the pitying sky.
As into air the purer spirits flow,
And separate from their kindred dregs below,
So flew the soul to its congenial place,
Nor left one virtue to redeem her race.
But thou, false guardian of a charge too good;
Thou, mean deserter of thy brother's blood !
See on these ruby lips the trembling breath,
These cheeks now fading at the blast of Death:
Cold is that breast which warm'd the world before,
And those love-darting eyes must roll no more.

252

Thus, if eternal justice rules the ball,
Thus shall your wives, and thus your children fall;
On all the line a sudden vengeance waits,
And frequent herses shall besiege your gates.
There passengers shall stand, and pointing say
(While the long fun'rals blacken all the way),
" Lo ! these were they whose souls the Furies steel'd
And cursed with hearts unknowing how to yield."
Thus unlamented pass the proud away,
The gaze of fools, and pageant of a day !
So perish all whose breast ne'er learned to glow
For others' good, or melt at others' woe !

What can atone (O ever-injured shade !)
Thy fate unpitied, and thy rites unpaid ?
No friend's complaint, no kind domestic tear
Pleased thy pale ghost, or graced thy mournful bier
By foreign hands thy dying eyes were closed,
By foreign hands thy decent limbs composed,
By foreign hands thy humble grave adorned,
By strangers honoured, and by strangers mourned !
What though no friends in sable weeds appear,
Grieve for an hour perhaps, then mourn a year,
And bear about the mockery of woe
To midnight dances, and the public show ?
What though no weeping Loves thy ashes grace,
Nor polished marble emulate thy face ?
What though no sacred earth allow thee room,
Nor hallowed dirge be muttered o'er thy tomb ?
Yet shall thy grave with rising flowers be drest,
And the green turf lie lightly on thy breast:

There shall the morn her earliest tears bestow,
There the first roses of the year shall blow;
While angels with their silver wings o'ershade
The ground now sacred by thy reliques made.
So peaceful rests, without a stone, a name,
What once had beauty, titles, wealth, and fame.
How loved, how honoured once, avails thee not,
To whom related, or by whom begot;
A heap of dust alone remains of thee,
'Tis all thou art, and all the proud shall be !
Poets themselves must fall, like those they sung,
Deaf the praised ear, and mute the tuneful tongue.
Even he, whose soul now melts in mournful lays,
Shall shortly want the generous tear he pays;
Then from his closing eyes thy form shall part,
And the last pang shall tear thee from his heart;
Life's idle business at one gasp be o'er,
The Muse forgot, and thou beloved no more !

ALEXANDER POPE

The Paragon of Animals

KNOW then thyself, presume not God to scan,
The proper study of mankind is man.
Placed on this isthmus of a middle state,
A being darkly wise, and rudely great.
With too much knowledge for the sceptic side,
With too much weakness for the stoic's pride,
He hangs between; in doubt to act, or rest;
In doubt to deem himself a god, or beast;
In doubt his mind or body to prefer;
Born but to die, and reasoning but to err;
Alike in ignorance, his reason such,
Whether he thinks too little or too much:
Chaos of Thought and Passion, all confused;
Still by himself abused or disabused;
Created half to rise and half to fall;
Great lord of all things, yet a prey to all;
Sole judge of truth, in endless error hurl'd:
The glory, jest, and riddle of the world !

(*From " The Essay on Man*"

ALEXANDER POPE

The Rape of the Lock

ON her white breast a sparkling Cross she wore
Which Jews might kiss and Infidels adore.
Her lively looks a sprightly mind disclose,
Quick as her eyes and as unfixed as those:
Favours to none, to all she smiles extends,
Oft she rejects, but never once offends. . . .
This Nymph, to the destruction of Mankind,
Nourished two Locks, which graceful hung behind
In equal curls, and well conspired to deck
With shining Ringlets the smooth ivory neck.
Love in these Labyrinths his slaves detains,
And mighty Hearts are held in slender chains.
With hairy springes we the birds betray,
Slight lines of Hair surprise the finny prey,
Fair tresses man's Imperial race insnare,
And beauty draws us with a single hair.

(From " The Rape of the Lock.")

ALEXANDER POPE

The Pleasure of Hope

HOPE springs eternal in the human breast;
Man never is, but always to be blest.
The soul, uneasy and confined from home,
Rests and expatiates in a life to come.

(From " The Essay or Man.")

For One who would not be Buried in Westminster Abbey

HEROES and kings ! your distance keep:
In peace let one poor poet sleep,
Who never flatter'd folks like you:
Let Horace blush, and Virgil too.

ALEXANDER GEDDES, Priest

(1737-1802)

Satire

SATIRE, my friend ('twixt me and you),
Can never please but very few.
The reason if you ask—'Tis plain, sir!
The most of mankind merit censure.
Th' ambitious knave, the wealthy fool,
Corruption's tamperer and tool;
The slave of luxury and lust,
The virtuoso mad for rust;
The trader, whose insatiate soul
Drives him like dust from pole to pole—
All these with one accord (you know it)
Dread poetry, and damn the poet.

THE CATHOLIC REVIVAL

JOHN HENRY NEWMAN, CARDINAL PRIEST

(1801–1890)

England

TYRE of the West, and glorying in the name
    More than in Faith's pure fame !
O trust not crafty fort nor rock renown'd
    Earn'd upon hostile ground ;
Wielding Trade's master-keys, at thy proud will
To lock or loose its waters, England ! trust not still.

Dread thine own power ! Since haughty Babel's prime,
    High towers have been man's crime.
Since her hoar age, when the huge moat lay bare,
    Strongholds have been man's snare.
Thy nest is in the crags ; ah ! refuge frail !
Mad counsel in its hour, or traitors, will prevail.

He who scann'd Sodom for His righteous men
    Still spares thee for thy ten ;
But, should vain tongues the Bride of Heaven defy,
    He will not pass thee by ;
For, as earth's kings welcome their spotless guest,
So gives He them by turn, to suffer or be blest.

JOHN HENRY NEWMAN

Judaism

(A Tragic Chorus)

O PITEOUS race !
　　Fearful to look upon,
Once standing in high place,
　　Heaven's eldest son.
　　O aged blind
Unvenerable ! as thou flittest by,
I liken thee to him in pagan song,
　　In thy gaunt majesty,
The vagrant King, of haughty-purposed mind
　　Whom prayer nor plague could bend;
Wrong'd, at the cost of him who did the wrong ;
Accursed himself, but in his cursing strong,
　　And honour'd in his end.

　　　O Abraham ! sire,
　　Shamed in thy progeny;
　　Who to thy faith aspire,
　　　Thy Hope deny.
　　　Well wast thou given
From out the heathen an adopted heir,
Raised strangely from the dead when sin had slain
　　Thy former-cherish'd care.
O holy men, ye first-wrought gems of heaven !
　　Polluted in your kin,
Come to our fonts, your lustre to regain.
O Holiest Lord ! . . . but Thou canst take no stain
　　Of blood, or taint of sin.

262

JOHN HENRY NEWMAN

Twice in their day
Proffer of precious cost
Was made, Heaven's hand to stay
Ere all was lost.
The first prevail'd;
Moses was outcast from the promised home
For his own sin, yet taken at his own prayer
To change his own people's doom.
Close on their eve, one other ask'd and fail'd;
When fervent Paul was fain
The accursèd tree, as Christ had borne, to bear,
No hopeful answer came,—a Price more rare
Already shed in vain.

JOHN HENRY NEWMAN

The Dream of Gerontius

GERONTIUS:

JESU, MARIA—I am near to death,
 And Thou art calling me; I know it now—
Not by the token of this faltering breath,
 This chill at heart, this dampness on my brow.
(Jesu, have mercy!   Mary, pray for me!)—
 'Tis this new feeling, never felt before,
(Be with me, Lord, in my extremity!)
That I am going, that I am no more.
'Tis this strange innermost abandonment,
 (Lover of souls! great God! I look to Thee.)
This emptying out of each constituent
 And natural force, by which I come to be.
Pray for me, O my friends; a visitant
 Is knocking his dire summons at my door,
The like of whom, to scare me and to daunt,
 Has never, never come to me before;
'Tis death—O loving friends, your prayers!—'tis he! . . .
 As though my very being had given way,
As though I was no more a substance now,
And could fall back on nought to be my stay,
 (Help, loving Lord!   Thou my sole refuge, Thou,)
And turn no whither, but must needs decay
 And drop from out the universal frame
Into that shapeless, scopeless, blank abyss,
 That utter nothingness, of which I came:
This is it that has come to pass in me;
O horror! this it is, my dearest, this;
So pray for me, my friends, who have not strength to pray.

JOHN HENRY NEWMAN

The Pillar of the Cloud

LEAD, kindly Light, through the encircling gloom;
    Lead Thou me on !
The night is dark, and I am far from home;
    Lead Thou me on !
Keep Thou my feet: I do not ask to see
The distant scene; one step enough for me.

I was not ever thus, nor prayed that Thou
    Shouldst lead me on.
I loved to choose and see my path; but now
    Lead Thou me on !
I loved the garish day, and, spite of fears,
Pride ruled my will; remember not past years.

So long Thy power hath blessed me, sure it still
    Shall lead me on
O'er moor and fen, o'er crag and torrent, till
    The night is gone,
And in the morn those angel faces smile
Whom I have loved long since, and lost awhile.

ROBERT STEPHEN HAWKER

(1803–1875)

Aishah Shechinah[1]

A SHAPE, like folded light, embodied air,
    Yet wreathed with flesh, and warm;
All that of Heaven is feminine and fair,
    Moulded in visible form.

She stood, the Lady Shechinah of Earth,
    A chancel for the sky;—
Where woke, to breath and beauty, God's own birth
    For men to see Him by.

Round her, too pure to mingle with the day,
    Light, that was Life, abode;
Folded within her fibres meekly lay
    The link of boundless God.

So linked, so blent, that when, with pulse fulfilled,
    Moved but that infant Hand,
Far, far away, His conscious Godhead thrilled,
    And stars might understand.

Lo ! where they pause, with intergathering rest,
    The Threefold and the One !
And lo ! He binds them to her Orient breast,
    His Manhood girded on.

The Zone, where two glad worlds for ever meet,
    Beneath that bosom ran:
Deep in that womb, the conquering Paraclete
    Smote Godhead on to man !

[1] Symbolic Hebraisms denoting Our Lady as the Pillar of Cloud.

ROBERT STEPHEN HAWKER

Sole scene among the stars; where, yearning, glide
The Threefold and the One:
Her God upon her lap: the Virgin-Bride,
Her awful Child: her Son.

ROBERT STEPHEN HAWKER

Trelawny

A GOOD sword and a trusty hand !
A merry heart and true !
King James' men shall understand
What Cornish lads can do.

And have they fixed the where and when ?
And shall Trelawny die ?
Here's twenty thousand Cornish men
Will know the reason why !

Out spake their captain brave and bold,
A merry wight was he:
·' If London Tower were Michael's hold,
We'll set Trelawny free !

" We'll cross the Tamar, land to land,
The Severn is no stay,
With ' one and all,' and hand in hand,
And who shall bid us nay ?

" And when we come to London Wall,
A pleasant sight to view,
Come forth ! come forth, ye cowards all,
Here's men as good as you !

" Trelawny he's in keep and hold,
Trelawny he may die:
But here's twenty thousand Cornish bold,
Will know the reason why !"

ROBERT STEPHEN HAWKER

A Christ-Cross Rhyme

CHRIST, His Cross shall be my speed !
　　Teach me, Father John, to read:
That in Church on Holy Day
I may chant the Psalm and pray.

Let me learn that I may know
What the shining windows show:
Where the lovely Lady stands,
With that bright Child in her hands.

Teach me the letters A B C
Till that I shall able be
Signs to know and words to frame
And to spell sweet Jesus' Name.

Then, dear Master, will I look
Day and night in that fair book
Where the tales of Saints are told
With their pictures all in gold.

Teach me, Father John, to say
Vesper-verse and Matin-lay:
So when I to God shall plead,
Christ His Cross shall be my speed !

FREDERICK WILLIAM FABER, Priest

(1814–1863)

The Expectation

ON the mountains of Judea,
    Like the chariot of the Lord,
Thou wert lifted in thy spirit
    By the uncreated Word;
Gifts and graces flowed upon thee
    In a sweet celestial strife,
And the growing of the Burden
    Was the lightening of thy life.

And what wonders have been in thee
    All the day and all the night,
While the angels fell before thee,
    To adore the Light of Light.
While the glory of the Father
    Hath been in thee as a home,
And the sceptre of creation
    Hath been wielded in thy womb.

And the sweet strains of the Psalmist
    Were a joy beyond control,
And the visions of the prophets
    Burnt like transports in thy soul;
But the Burden that was growing,
    And was felt so tenderly,
It was Heaven, it was Heaven,
    Come before its time to thee.

              (From " Our Lady's Expectation.")

FREDERICK WILLIAM FABER

Our Lady in the Middle Ages

I LOOKED upon the earth: it was a floor
   For noisy pageant and rude bravery—
Wassail, and arms, and chase, among the high,
And burning hearts uncheered among the poor;
And gentleness from every land withdrew.
Methought that beds of whitest lilies grew
All suddenly upon the earth, in bowers;
And gentleness, that wandered like a wind,
And nowhere could meet sanctuary find,
Passed like a dewy breath into the flowers.
Earth heeded not; she still was tributary
To kings and knights, and man's heart well-nigh failed;
Then were the natural charities exhaled
Afresh, from out the blessed love of Mary.

FREDERICK WILLIAM FABER

"*Mundus Morosus*"

I HEARD the wild beasts in the wood complain;
Some slept, while others wakened to sustain
Through night and day the sad monotonous round
Half savage and half pitiful the sound.

The outcry rose to God through all the air,
The worship of distress, an animal prayer,
Loud vehement pleadings, not unlike to those
Job uttered in his agony of woes.

The very pauses, when they came, were rife
With sickening sounds of too successful strife;
As when the clash of battle dies away,
The groans of night succeed the shrieks of day.

Man's scent the untamed creatures scarce can bear,
As if his tainted blood defiled the air;
In the vast woods they fret as in a cage,
Or fly in fear, or gnash their teeth with rage.

The beasts of burden linger on their way,
Like slaves who will not speak when they obey;
Their faces, when their looks to us they raise,
With something of reproachful patience gaze.

All creatures round us seem to disapprove;
Their eyes discomfort us with lack of love;
Our very rights, with sighs like these alloyed,
Not without sad misgivings are enjoyed.

FREDERICK WILLIAM FABER

Mostly men's many-featured faces wear
Looks of fixed gloom, or else of restless care;
The very babes, that in their cradles lie,
Out of the depths of unknown trouble cry.

Labour itself is but a sorrowful song,
The protest of the weak against the strong;
Over rough waters, and in obstinate fields,
And from dank mines, the same sad sound it yields

Doth Earth send nothing up to Thee but moans.
Father? Canst Thou find melody in groans?
O, can it be that Thou, the God of bliss,
Canst feed Thy glory on a world like this?

Yet it is well with us. From these alarms
Like children scared we fly into Thine arms;
And pressing sorrows put our pride to rout
With a swift faith which has not time to doubt.

We cannot herd in peace with wild beasts rude;
We dare not live in Nature's solitude;
In how few eyes of men can we behold
Enough of love to make us calm and bold?

O, it is well with us! With angry glance
Life glares at us, or looks at us askance:
Seek where we will—Father, we see it now!—
None love us, trust us, welcome us, but Thou.

COVENTRY PATMORE

(1823–1896)

The Toys

MY little Son, who look'd from thoughtful eyes
    And moved and spoke in quiet grown-up wise,
Having my law the seventh time disobey'd,
I struck him, and dismiss'd
With hard words and unkiss'd.
. . . His Mother, who was patient, being dead.
Then, fearing lest his grief should hinder sleep,
I visited his bed,
But found him slumbering deep,
With darken'd eyelids, and their lashes yet
From his late sobbing wet.
And I, with moan,
Kissing away his tears, left others of my own;
For, on a table drawn beside his head,
He had put, within his reach,
A box of counters and a red-vein'd stone,
A piece of glass abraded by the beach,
And six or seven shells,
A bottle with bluebells,
And two French copper coins, ranged here with careful
    art,
To comfort his sad heart.
So when that night I pray'd
To God, I wept, and said:
Ah, when at last we lie with trancèd breath,
Not vexing Thee in death,
And Thou rememberest of what toys
We made our joys,

How weakly understood
Thy great commanded good,
Then, fatherly not less
Than I whom Thou hast moulded from the clay,
Thou'lt leave Thy wrath, and say,
" I will be sorry for their childishness."

A Farewell

WITH all my will, but much against my heart,
    We two now part.
My Very Dear,
    Our solace is, the sad road lies so clear.
It needs no art,
With faint, averted feet
    And many a tear,
In our opposed paths to persevere.
    Go thou to East, I West,
We will not say
There's any hope, it is so far away.
    But, O, my Best!
When the one darling of our widow-head,
    The nursling Grief,
Is dead,
And no dew blur our eyes
To see the peach-bloom come in evening skies,
    Perchance we may,
    Where now this night is day,
And even through faith of still averted feet,
    Making full circle of our banishment,
Amazed meet;
The bitter journey to the bourne so sweet
    Seasoning the termless feast of our content
With tears of recognition never dry.

COVENTRY PATMORE

" *If I were Dead* "

" IF I were dead, you'd sometimes say, Poor Child !"
 The dear lips quiver'd as they spake,
And the tears brake
From eyes which, not to grieve me, brightly miled.
Poor Child, poor Child !
I seem to hear your laugh, your talk, your song.
It is not true that Love will do no wrong.
Poor Child !
And did you think, when you so cried and smiled,
How I, in lonely nights, should lie . wake,
And of those words your full avengers make ?
Poor Child, poor Child !
And now, unless it be
That sweet amends thrice told are come to thee,
O God, have Thou *no* mercy upon me !
Poor Child !

Departure

IT was not like your great and gracious ways!
   Do you, that have naught other to lament,
Never, my Love, repent
Of how, that July afternoon,
You went,
With sudden, unintelligible phrase,
And frighten'd eye,
Upon your journey of so many days
Without a single kiss, or a good-bye?
I knew, indeed, that you were parting soon;
And so we sate, within the low sun's rays,
You whispering to me, for your voice was weak,
Your harrowing praise.
Well, it was well
To hear you such things speak,
And I could tell
What made your eyes a growing gloom of love,
As a warm South wind sombres a March grove.
And it was like your great and gracious ways
To turn your talk on daily things, my Dear,
Lifting the luminous, pathetic lash
To let the laughter flash,
Whilst I drew near,
Because you spoke so low that I could scarcely hear.
But all at once to leave me at the last,
More at the wonder than the loss aghast,
With huddled, unintelligible phrase,
And frighten'd eye,

And go your journey of all days
With not one kiss, or a good-bye,
And the only loveless look, the look with which you
    passed:
'Twas all unlike your great and gracious ways.

Auras of Delight

BEAUTIFUL habitations, auras of delight!
　　Who shall bewail the crags and bitter foam
And angry sword-blades flashing left and right
Which guard your glittering height,
That none thereby may come!
The vision which we have
Revere we so,
That yet we crave
To foot those fields of ne'er profanèd snow? . . .
And Him I thank, who can make live again
The dust, but not the joy we once profane,
That I, of ye,
Beautiful habitations, auras of delight,
In childish years and since had sometime sense and
　　　sight,
But that ye vanish'd quite,
Even from memory,
Ere I could get my breath, and whisper " See!"
　　But did for me
They altogether die,
Those trackless glories glimps'd in upper sky?
Were they of chance, or vain,
Nor good at all again
For curb of heart or fret?
Nay, though, by grace,
Lest haply I refuse God to His face,
Their likeness wholly I forget,
Ah! yet,

Often in straits which else for me were ill,
I mind me still
I *did* respire the lonely auras sweet,
I *did* the blest abodes behold, and, at the mountains' feet
Bathed in the holy Stream by Hermon's thymy hill.

GERARD HOPKINS, JESUIT

(1844–1889)

Barnfloor and Winepress

THOU who on Sin's wages starvest,
   Behold we have the Joy of Harvest:
For us was gathered the First-fruits,
For us was lifted from the roots,
Sheaved in cruel bands, bruisèd sore,
Scourged upon the threshing floor,
Where the upper millstone roofed His Head,
At morn we found the Heavenly Bread;
And on a thousand altars laid,
Christ our Sacrifice is made.

Thou, whose dry plot for moisture gapes,
We shout with them that tread the grapes;
For us the Vine was fenced with thorn,
Five ways the precious branches torn.
Terrible fruit was on the tree
In the acre of Gethsemane:
For us by Calvary's distress
The wine was rackèd from the press;
Now, in our altar-vessels stored,
Lo, the sweet vintage of the Lord!

In Joseph's garden they threw by
The riven Vine, leafless, lifeless, dry:
On Easter morn the Tree was forth,
In forty days reached Heaven from earth,—
Soon the whole world is overspread:
Ye weary, come into the shade.

GERARD HOPKINS

The field where He hath planted us
Shall shake her fruit as Libanus,
When He has sheaved us in His sheaf,
When He has made us bear His leaf.
We scarcely call that banquet food,
But even our Saviour's and our blood,
We are so grafted on His wood.

GERARD HOPKINS

Heaven Haven

(A Nun takes the Veil)

I HAVE desired to go
　　Where springs not fail,
To fields where flies no sharp and sided hail,
　　And a few lilies blow.

　　And I have asked to be
　　Where no storms come,
Where the green swell is in the havens dumb,
　　And out of the swing of the sea.

GERARD HOPKINS

The Starlight Night

LOOK at the stars ! Look, look up at the skies !
     O look at all the fire-folk sitting in the air !
  The bright bóroughs, the quivering citadels there !
The dim woods quick with diamond wells; the elf eyes !
The grey lawns cold where the quaking gold-dew lies !
  Wind-beat white-beam; airy abeles all on flare !
  Flake-doves sent floating out at a farmyard scare !—
Ah well ! it is a purchase and a prize.

Buy then ! Bid then !—What ?—Prayer, patience, alms,
     vows.—
  Look, look ! a May-mess, like on orchard boughs;
  Look ! March-bloom, like on mealed-with-yellow sallows.—
These are indeed the barn: within-doors house
The shocks.   This piece-bright paling hides the Spouse
  Christ, and the mother of Christ and all his hallows.

GERARD HOPKINS

The Windhover

I CAUGHT this morning morning's minion, King-
dom of daylight's dauphin, dapple-dawn-drawn Falcon,
in his riding
Of the rolling level underneath him steady air, and striding
High there, how he rung upon the rein of a wimpling wing
In his ecstasy ! then off, off forth on swing,
As a skate's heel sweeps smooth on a bow-bend: the hurl and
gliding
Rebuffed the big wind.   My heart in hiding
Stirred for a bird,—the achieve of, the mastery of the thing!

Brute beauty and valour and act, oh, air, pride, plume, here
Buckle ! and the fire that breaks from thee then, a billion
Times told lovelier, more dangerous, O my chevalier !

No wonder of it; shéer plód makes plough down sillion
Shine, and blue-beak embers, ah my dear,
Fall, gall themselves, and gash gold-vermilion.

GERARD HOPKINS

The Habit of Perfection

ELECTED Silence, sing to me
And beat upon my whorlèd ear,
Pipe me to pastures still and be
The music that I care to hear.

Shape nothing, lips; be lovely-dumb:
It is the shut, the curfew sent
From there where all surrenders come
Which only makes you eloquent.

Be shellèd, eyes, with double dark
And find the uncreated light:
This ruck and reel which you remark
Coils, keeps and teases simple sight.

Palate, the hutch of tasty lust,
Desire not to be rinsed with wine:
The can must be so sweet, the crust
So fresh that come in fasts divine !

Nostrils, your careless breath that spend
Upon the stir and keep of pride,
What relish shall the censers send
Along the sanctuary side !

O feel-of-primrose hands, O feet
That want the yield of plushy sward,
But you shall walk the golden street,
And you unhouse and house the Lord.

And, Poverty, be thou the bride
And now the marriage feast begun,
And lily-coloured clothes provide
Your spouse not laboured-at, nor spun.

GERARD HOPKINS

Inversnaid

THIS darksome burn, horse-back brown,
His rollrock highroad roaring down,
In coop and in comb the fleece of his foam
Flutes and low to the lake falls home.

A wind-puff-bonnet of fawn-froth
Turns and twindles over the broth
Of a pool so pitchblack, fell-frowning,
It rounds and rounds Despair to drowning.

Degged with dew, dappled with dew
Are the groins of the braes that the brook treads thro'
Wiry heathpacks, flitches of fern,
And the beadbonny ash that sits over the burn.

What would the world be, once bereft
Of wet and of wildness ? Let them be left,
O let them be left, wildness and wet;
Long live the weeds and the wilderness yet.

Rosa Mystica

"THE rose is a mystery"—where is it found?
 Is it anything true?   Does it grow upon ground?
It was made of earth's mould, but it went from men's eyes,
And its place is a secret and shut in the skies.

In the gardens of God, in the daylight divine,
Find me a place by thee, mother of mine.

But where was it formerly?   Which is the spot
That was blest in it once, though now it is not?
It is Galilee's growth: it grew at God's will
And broke into bloom upon Nazareth hill.

In the gardens of God, in the daylight divine,
I shall look on thy loveliness, mother of mine.

What was its season then?   How long ago?
When was the summer that saw the bud blow?
Two thousands of years are near upon past
Since its birth and its bloom and its breathing its last.

In the gardens of God, in the daylight divine,
I shall keep time with thee, mother of mine.

Tell me the name now, tell me its name.
The heart guesses easily: is it the same?
Mary the Virgin, well the heart knows,
She is the mystery, she is that rose.

In the gardens of God, in the daylight divine,
I shall come home to thee, mother of mine.

289

Is Mary the rose then? Mary, the tree?
But the blossom, the blossom there—who can it be?
Who can her rose be? It could but be One
Christ Jesus our Lord, her God and her son.
        In the gardens of God, in the daylight divine,
        Show me thy son, mother, mother of mine.

What was the colour of that blossom bright?—
White to begin with, immaculate white.
But what a wild flush on the flakes of it stood
When the rose ran in crimsonings down the cross-wood!
        In the gardens of God, in the daylight divine
        I shall worship His wounds with thee, mother of mine

How many leaves had it?—Five they were then,
Five, like the senses and members of men;
Five is their number by nature, but now
They multiply, multiply—who can tell how?
        In the gardens of God, in the daylight divine
        Make me a leaf in thee, mother of mine.

Does it smell sweet, too, in that holy place?
Sweet unto God and the sweetness is grace:
The breath of it bathes great heaven above
In grace that is charity, grace that is love.
        To thy breast, to thy rest, to thy glory divine
        Draw me by charity, mother of mine.

JOHN BANISTER TABB, Priest

(1845–1909)

The Reaper

TELL me whither, maiden June,
Down the dusky slope of noon,
With thy sickle of a moon,
Goest thou to reap.

" Fields of Fancy by the stream
Of night in silvery silence gleam,
To heap with many a harvest-dream
The granary of Sleep."

JOHN BANISTER TABB

Father Damien

O GOD, the cleanest offering
  Of tainted earth below,
Unblushing to thy feet we bring—
" A leper white as snow !"

Betrayal

" WHOM I shall kiss," I heard a Sunbeam say,
    " Take him and lead away !"
Then, with the Traitor's salutation, " Hail !"
He kissed the Dawn-Star pale.

JOHN BANISTER TABB

The Water-Lily

WHENCE, O fragrant form of light,
   Hast thou drifted through the night,
Swanlike, to a leafy nest,
On the restless waves, at rest?

Art thou from the snowy zone
Of a mountain-summit blown,
Or the blossom of a dream,
Fashioned in the foamy stream?

Nay, methinks the maiden moon,
When the daylight came too soon,
Fleeting from her bath to hide,
Left her garment in the tide.

FRANCIS THOMPSON

(1860–1907)

The Hound of Heaven

I FLED Him, down the nights and down the days;
 I fled Him, down the arches of the years;
I fled Him, down the labyrinthine ways
 Of my own mind; and in the mist of tears
I hid from Him, and under running laughter.
   Up vistaed hopes I sped;
   And shot, precipitated,
Adown Titanic glooms of chasmèd fears,
 From those strong Feet that followed, followed after.

   But with unhurrying chase,
   And unperturbèd pace,
 Deliberate speed, majestic instancy,
   They beat—and a Voice beat
   More instant than the Feet—
 " All things betray thee, who betrayest Me."

   I pleaded, outlaw-wise,
By many a hearted casement, curtained red,
 Trellised with intertwining charities
(For, though I knew His love Who followèd,
   Yet was I sore adread
Lest, having Him, I must have naught beside);
But, if one little casement parted wide,
 The gust of His approach would clash it to.
 Fear wist not to evade as Love wist to pursue.
Across the margent of the world I fled,
 And troubled the gold gateways of the stars,
 Smiting for shelter on their clangèd bars;
   Fretted to dulcet jars

And silvern chatter the pale ports o' the moon.
I said to dawn: Be sudden; to eve: Be soon;
  With thy young skiey blossoms heap me over
    From this tremendous Lover!
Float thy vague veil about me, lest He see!
  I tempted all His servitors, but to find
  My own betrayal in their constancy,
  In faith to Him their fickleness to me,
    Their traitorous trueness, and their loyal deceit.
To all swift things for swiftness did I sue;
  Clung to the whistling mane of every wind.
    But whether they swept, smoothly fleet,
      The long savannahs of the blue;
        Or whether, Thunder-driven,
      They clanged His chariot 'thwart a heaven,
Plashy with flying lightnings round the spurn o' their feet:—
Fear wist not to evade as Love wist to pursue.

      Still with unhurrying chase,
      And unperturbèd pace,
    Deliberate speed, majestic instancy,
      Came on the following Feet,
      And a Voice above their beat—
    " Naught shelters thee, who wilt not shelter Me."

I sought no more that after which I strayed
      In face of man or maid;
But still within the little children's eyes
    Seems something, something that replies,
They at least are for me, surely for me!
I turned me to them very wistfully;
But, just as their young eyes grew sudden fair
      With dawning answers there,

Their angel plucked them from me by the hair.
" Come then, ye other children, Nature's—share
With me " (said I) " your delicate fellowship;
     Let me greet you lip to lip,
     Let me twine with you caresses,
        Wantoning
     With our Lady-Mother's vagrant tresses,
        Banqueting
     With her in her wind-walled palace,
     Underneath her azured daïs,
     Quaffing, as your taintless way is,
        From a chalice
Lucent-weeping out of the dayspring."
        So it was done:
I in their delicate fellowship was one—
Drew the bolt of Nature's secrecies.
     I knew all the swift importings
     On the wilful face of skies;
     I knew how the clouds arise,
     Spumèd of the wild sea-snortings;
        All that's born or dies
     Rose and drooped with; made them shapers
Of mine own moods, or wailful or divine—
     With them joyed and was bereaven.
     I was heavy with the even,
     When she lit her glimmering tapers
     Round the day's dead sanctities.
     I laughed in the morning's eyes.
I triumphed and I saddened with all weather,
     Heaven and I wept together,
And its sweet tears were salt with mortal mine;
Against the red throb of its sunset-heart

I laid my own to beat,
And share commingling heat;
But not by that, by that, was eased my human smart.
In vain my tears were wet on Heaven's grey cheek.
For ah ! we know not what each other says,
These things and I; in sound *I* speak—
Their sound is but their stir, they speak by silences.
Nature, poor stepdame, cannot slake my drouth;
Let her, if she would owe me,
Drop yon blue bosom-veil of sky, and show me
The breasts o' her tenderness:
Never did any milk of hers once bless
My thirsting mouth.

Nigh and nigh draws the chase,
With unperturbèd pace,
Deliberate speed, majestic instancy,
And past those noisèd Feet
A Voice comes yet more fleet—
" Lo! naught contents thee, who content'st not Me."

Naked I wait Thy love's uplifted stroke !
My harness piece by piece Thou hast hewn from me,
And smitten me to my knee;
I am defenceless utterly.
I slept, methinks, and woke,
And, slowly gazing, find me stripped in sleep.
In the rash lustihead of my young powers,
I shook the pillaring hours
And pulled my life upon me; grimed with smears,
I stand amid the dust o' the mounded years—
My mangled youth lies dead beneath the heap.
My days have crackled and gone up in smoke,

Have puffed and burst as sun-starts on a stream.
        Yea, faileth now even dream
The dreamer, and the lute the lutanist;
Even the linked fantasies, in whose blossomy twist
I swung the earth a trinket at my wrist,
Are yielding; cords of all too weak account
For earth, with heavy griefs so overplussed.
        Ah! is Thy love indeed
A weed, albeit an amaranthine weed,
Suffering no flowers except its own to mount?
        Ah! must—
        Designer infinite!—
Ah! must Thou char the wood ere Thou canst limn with it?
My freshness spent its wavering shower i' the dust;
And now my heart is as a broken fount,
Wherein tear-drippings stagnate, spilt down ever
        From the dank thoughts that shiver
Upon the sighful branches of my mind.
        Such is; what is to be?
The pulp so bitter, how shall taste the rind?
I dimly guess what Time in mists confounds;
Yet ever and anon a trumpet sounds
From the hid battlements of Eternity;
Those shaken mists a space unsettle, then
Round the half-glimpsèd turrets slowly wash again.
        But not ere him who summoneth
        I first have seen, enwound
With glooming robes purpureal, cypress-crowned;
His name I know, and what his trumpet saith.
Whether man's heart or life it be which yields
        Thee harvest, must Thy harvest fields
        Be dunged with rotten death?

Now of that long pursuit
Comes on at hand the bruit;
That Voice is round me like a bursting sea:
" And is thy earth so marred,
Shattered in shard on shard?
Lo, all things fly thee, for thou fliest Me!
Strange, piteous, futile thing,
Wherefore should any set thee love apart?
Seeing none but I makes much of naught " (He said),
" And human love needs human meriting:
How hast thou merited—
Of all man's clotted clay the dingiest clot?
Alack, thou knowest not
How little worthy of any love thou art!
Whom wilt thou find to love ignoble thee,
Save Me, save only Me?
All which I took from thee I did but take,
Not for thy harms,
But just that thou might'st seek it in My arms.
All which thy child's mistake
Fancies as lost, I have stored for thee at home:
Rise, clasp My hand, and come."

Halts by me that footfall:
Is my gloom, after all,
Shade of His hand, outstretched caressingly?
" Ah, fondest, blindest, weakest,
I am He Whom thou seekest!
Thou dravest love from thee, who dravest Me "

ROBERT HUGH BENSON, Priest
(1871–1914)

The Priest's Lament

LORD, hast Thou set me here
    Thy priest to be,
The burden of Thy yoke to bear,
To feel Thy cords about me set,
Wince at the lash, but never yet
    Thy Face to see?

Lord, see what wounds on me
    Thy burden makes!
Dost Thou despise my misery?
Ah, Master! Wilt Thou let me strain,
And fall and rise and fall again,
    Till my heart breaks?

Lord, I am near to die,
    So steep the hill,
So slow the wheels, so feeble I,
The halting place so far above.
Art Thou indeed a God of Love,
    And tender still?

" Son, turn a moment, see
    Is that blood thine?
Who is it shares thy yoke with thee,
Treads foot by foot with thee the road?
Whose shoulder bears the heavier load,—
    Is it not Mine?"

ROBERT HUGH BENSON

The Teresian Contemplative

SHE moves in tumult; round her lies
   The silence of the world of grace;
The twilight of our mysteries
   Shines like high noonday on her face;
Our piteous guesses, dim with fears,
She touches, handles, sees, and hears.

In her all longings mix and meet;
   Dumb souls through her are eloquent;
She feels the world beneath her feet
   Thrill in a passionate intent;
Through her our tides of feeling roll
And find their God within her soul.

Her faith the awful Face of God
   Brightens and blinds with utter light;
Her footsteps fall where late He trod;
   She sinks in roaring voids of night;
Cries to her Lord in black despair,
And knows, yet knows not, He is there.

A willing sacrifice she takes
   The burden of our fall within;
Holy she stands; while on her breaks
   The lightning of the wrath of sin;
She drinks her Saviour's cup of pain,
And, one with Jesus, thirsts again.

THE HOLY WOMEN

ADELAIDE ANNE PROCTER

(1825–1864)

Give Me Thy Heart

WITH echoing step the worshippers
    Departed one by one;
The organ's pealing voice was stilled,
    The vesper hymn was done;
The shadows fell from roof and arch,
    Dim was the incensed air,
One lamp alone with trembling ray,
    Told of the Presence there !

In the dark church she knelt alone;
    Her tears were falling fast;
" Help, Lord," she cried, " the shades of death
    Upon my soul are cast !
Have I not shunned the path of sin
    And chosen the better part ?"
What voice came through the sacred air ?
    '· My child, give me thy heart !"

For I have loved thee with a love
    No mortal heart can show;
A love so deep, My Saints in Heaven
    Its depths can never know:
When pierced and wounded on the Cross,
    Man's sin and doom were Mine,
I love l thee with undying love;
    Immortal and divine.

In awe she listened and the shade
Passed from her soul away;
In low and trembling voice she cried,
"Lord, help me to obey !
Break Thou the chains of earth, O Lord,
That bind and hold my heart;
Let it be Thine and Thine alone,
Let none with Thee have part !"

MAY PROBYN

A Christmas Carol

LACKING samite and sable,
　　Lacking silver and gold,
The Prince Jesus in the poor stable
Slept, and was three hours old.

As doves by the fair water,
Mary, not touched of sin,
Sat by Him,—the King's daughter,
All glorious within.

A lily without one stain, a
Star where no spot hath room—
Ave, gratia plena,
Virgo Virginum.

Clad not in pearl-sewn vesture,
Clad not in cramoisie,
She hath hushed, she hath cradled to rest, her
God the first time on her knee.

Where is one to adore Him ?
The ox hath dumbly confessed,
With the ass, meek kneeling before Him,
" *Et homo factus est.*"

Not throned on ivory or cedar,
Not crowned with a Queen's crown,
At her breast it is Mary shall feed her
Maker, from Heaven come down.

MAY PROBYN

The trees in Paradise blossom
Sudden, and its bells chime—
She giveth Him, held to her bosom,
Her immaculate milk the first time.

The night with wings of angels
Was alight, and its snow-packed ways
Sweet made (say the Evangels)
With the noise of their virelays.

Quem vidistis, pastores?
Why go ye feet unshod ?
Wot ye within yon door is
Mary, the Mother of God ?

No smoke of spice ascending
There—no roses are piled—
But, choicer than all balms blending,
There Mary hath kissed her Child.

ELEANOR HAMILTON KING

(1840–1920)

The Garden of the Holy Souls

IN Thy garden, in Thy garden, though the rain
    Fall, and the winds beat there,
And they stand unsheltered, piteous, in the storm,
    They who were once so fair.

In Thy garden of the souls, where Thou art gardener,
    Thou who wast once so mild,
Now pruning down to naked stems and leafless
    The roses that ran wild.

Oh, Thy roses once waved in the wind so sweetly,
    Though thick with thorns beset;
In the morning sunshine opening, and at evening
    With cool dews wet.

In Thy garden, where Thou walkest as a warder,
    How poor, how small they stand;
Yet once their beauty, to the hearts that loved them,
    Lighted the living land.

In Thy garden, where no smile of Thine is granted,
    Yet keep within Thy heart,
A place in Paradise for these transplanted,
    Still with Thee where Thou art.

In Thy garden, in Thy garden, where Thy roses
    Without a thorn are sweet,
And each poor branch in endless wreaths uncloses
    To kiss Thy feet.

(From " Hours of the Passion.")

ALICE MEYNELL

Christ in the Universe

WITH this ambiguous earth
  His dealings have been told us. These abide:
The signal to a maid, the human birth,
The lesson, and the young Man crucified.

But not a star of all
The innumerable host of stars has heard
How He administered this terrestrial ball.
Our race have kept their Lord's entrusted Word.

Of His earth-visiting feet
None knows the secret, cherished, perilous,
The terrible, shamefast, frightened, whispered, sweet,
Heart-shattering secret of His way with us.

No planet knows that this
Our wayside, carrying land and wave,
Love and life multiplied, and pain and bliss,
Bears, as chief treasure, one forsaken grave.

Nor, in our little day,
May His devices with the heavens be guessed,
His pilgrimage to thread the Milky Way,
Or His bestowals there be manifest.

But in the eternities
Doubtless we shall compare together, hear
A million alien Gospels, in what guise
He trod the Pleiades, the Lyre, the Bear.

O, be prepared, my soul,
To read the inconceivable, to scan
The million forms of God those stars unroll
When, in our turn, we show to them a Man.

ALICE MEYNELL

The Young Neophyte

WHO knows what days I answer for to-day ?
    Giving the bud I give the flower.   I bow
This yet unfaded and a faded brow;
Bending these knees and feeble knees, I pray.
Thoughts yet unripe in me I bend one way,
Give one repose to pain I know not now,
One check to joy that comes, I guess not how.
I dedicate my fields when Spring is grey.
O rash ! (I smile) to pledge my hidden wheat.
I fold to-day at altars far apart
Hands trembling with what toils ?   In their retreat
I seal my love to-be, my folded art.
I light the tapers at my head and feet,
And lay the crucifix on this silent heart.

ALICE MEYNELL

The Shepherdess

SHE walks—the lady of my delight—
  A shepherdess of sheep.
Her flocks are thoughts, she keeps them white;
She guards from the steep;
She feeds them on the fragrant height,
And folds them in for sleep.

She roams maternal hills and bright,
Dark valleys safe and deep.
Into that tender breast at night
The chastest stars may peep.
She walks—the lady of my delight—
A shepherdess of sheep.

She holds her little thoughts in sight,
Though gay they run and leap,
She is so circumspect and right;
She has her soul to keep.
She walks—the lady of my delight—
A shepherdess of sheep.

ALICE MEYNELL

Thoughts in Separation

WE never meet; yet we meet day by day
    Upon those hills of life, dim and immense—
The good we love, and sleep, our innocence,
O hills of life, high hills ! And, higher than they,
Our guardian spirits meet at prayer and play.
Beyond pain, joy, and hope, and long suspense,
Above the summits of our souls, far hence,
An angel meets an angel on the way.
Beyond all good I ever believed of thee,
Or thou of me, these always love and live.
And though I fail of thy ideal of me,
My angel falls not short. They greet each other.
Who knows, they may exchange the kiss we give
Thou to thy crucifix, I to my mother.

ALICE MEYNELL

"*I am the Way*"

THOU art the Way.
  Hadst Thou been nothing but the goal,
I cannot say
If Thou hadst ever met my soul.

I cannot see—
I, child of process—if there lies
An end for me,
Full of repose, full of replies.

I'll not reproach
The road that winds, my feet that err.
Access, Approach
Art Thou, Time, Way, and Wayfarer.

To the Body

THOU inmost, ultimate
 Council of judgement, palace of decrees,
Where the high senses hold their spiritual state,
Sued by earth's embassies,
And sign, approve, accept, conceive, create.

Create—thy senses close
With the world's pleas. The random odours reach
Their sweetness in the place of thy repose,
Upon thy tongue the peach,
And in thy nostrils breathes the breathing rose.

To thee, secluded one,
The dark vibrations of the sightless skies,
The lovely inexplicit colours run;
The light gropes for those eyes.
O thou august ! thou dost command the sun.

Music, all dumb, hath trod
Into thine ear her one effectual way;
And fire and cold approach to gain thy nod,
Where thou call'st up the day,
Where thou awaitest the appeal of God.

DORA SIGERSON SHORTER

Sixteen Dead Men

H ARK ! in the still night. Who goes there ?
 " *Fifteen dead men.*" Why do they wait ?
" *Hasten, comrade, death is so fair.*"
 Now comes their Captain through the dim gate.

Sixteen dead men ! What on their sword ?
 " *A nation's honour proud do they bear.*"
What on their bent heads ? " *God's holy word ;*
 All of their nation's heart blended in prayer."

Sixteen dead men ! What makes their shroud ?
 " *All of their nation's love wraps them around.*"
Where do their bodies lie, brave and so proud ?
 " *Under the gallows-tree in prison ground.*"

Sixteen dead men ! Where do they go ?
 " *To join their regiment, where Sarsfield leads ;*
Wolfe Tone and Emmet, too, well do they know.
 There shall they bivouac, telling great deeds."

Sixteen dead men ! Shall they return ?
 " *Yea, they shall come again, breath of our breath.*
They on our nation's hearth made old fires burn.
 Guard her unconquered soul, strong in their death."

THE IRISH

THOMAS MOORE

(1779–1852)

The Harp that Once through Tara's Halls

THE harp that once through Tara's halls
    The soul of music shed,
Now hangs as mute on Tara's walls
    As if that soul were fled.
So sleeps the pride of former days,
    So glory's thrill is o'er,
And hearts that once beat high for praise
    Now feel that pulse no more.

No more to chiefs and ladies bright
    The harp of Tara swells:
The chord alone that breaks at night
    Its tale of ruin tells.
Thus Freedom now so seldom wakes,
    The only throb she gives
Is when some heart, indignant, breaks,
    To show that she still lives.

THOMAS MOORE

The Irish Peasant to his Mistress

THROUGH grief and through danger thy smile hath
cheered my way,
'Till hope seem'd to bud from each thorn that round me lay;
The darker our fortune, the brighter our pure love burn'd,
Till shame into glory, till fear into zeal was turn'd;
Yes, slave as I was, in thy arms my spirit felt free,
And bless'd even the sorrows that made me more dear to thee.

Thy rival was honour'd, while thou wert wrong'd and
scorn'd,
Thy crown was of briers, while gold her brows adorn'd;
She woo'd me to temples, while thou lay'st hid in caves,
Her friends were all masters, while thine, alas! were slaves;
Yet cold in the earth, at thy feet, I would rather be,
Than wed what I lov'd not, or turn one thought from thee.

They slander thee sorely, who say thy vows are frail—
Hadst thou been a false one, thy cheek had look'd less pale.
They say, too, so long thou hast worn those lingering chains,
That deep in thy heart they have printed their servile stains—
Oh! foul is the slander—no chain could that soul subdue—
Where shineth thy spirit, there liberty shineth too!

THOMAS MOORE

The Minstrel-Boy

THE Minstrel-Boy to the war is gone,
   In the ranks of death you'll find him;
His father's sword he has girded on,
   And his wild harp slung behind him.
" Land of song !" said the warrior-bard,
   " Tho' all the world betrays thee,
One sword, at least, thy rights shall guard,
   One faithful harp shall praise thee !"

The Minstrel fell !—but the foeman's chain
   Could not bring his proud soul under;
The harp he lov'd ne'er spoke again,
   For he tore its chords asunder;
And said, " No chains shall sully thee,
   Thou soul of love and bravery !
Thy songs were made for the pure and free,
   They shall never sound in slavery."

GERALD GRIFFIN

(1803–1840)

I Love my Love in the Morning

I LOVE my Love in the morning,
    For she like morn is fair—
Her blushing cheek its crimson streak,
    Its clouds her golden hair,
Her glance its beam so soft and kind,
    Her tears its dewy showers,
And her voice the tender whispering wind
    That stirs the early bowers.

I love my Love in the morning,
    I love my Love at noon,
For she is bright as the lord of light,
    Yet mild as Autumn's moon.
Her beauty is my bosom's sun,
    Her faith my fostering shade,
And I will love my darling one
    Till ever the sun shall fade.

I love my Love in the morning,
    I love my Love at even;
Her smile's soft play is like the ray
    That lights the western heaven.
I loved her when the sun was high,
    I loved her when he rose,
But best of all when evening's sigh
    Was murmuring at its close.

GERALD GRIFFIN

O Brazil, the Isle of the Blest

ON the ocean that hollows the rocks where ye dwell,
  A shadowy land has appeared as they tell;
Men thought it a region of sunshine and rest,
And they called it O Brazil, the isle of the blest.
From year unto year, on the ocean's blue rim,
The beautiful spectre showed lovely and dim;
The golden clouds curtained the deep where it lay,
And it looked like an Eden, away, far away!

A peasant who heard of the wonderful tale,
In the breeze of the Orient, loosened his sail;
From Ara, the holy, he turned to the west,
For though Ara was holy, O Brazil was blest.
He heard not the voices that called from the shore,
He heard not the rising wind's menacing roar;
Home kindred and safety he left on that day,
And he sped to O Brazil, away, far away!

Morn rose on the deep, and that shadowy isle
O'er the faint rim of distance reflected its smile;
Noon burned on the wave, and that shadowy shore
Seemed lovelily distant, and faint as before:
Lone evening came down on the wanderer's track,
And to Ara again he looked timidly back;
Oh, far on the verge of the ocean it lay,
Yet the isle of the blest was away, far away!

Rash dreamer, return !   O ye winds of the main,
Bear him back to his own peaceful Ara again;
Rash fool, for a vision of fanciful bliss,
To barter thy calm life of labour and peace.
The warning of Reason was spoken in vain,
He never revisited Ara again ;
Night fell on the deep, amidst tempest and spray,
And he died on the waters, away, far away !

JAMES CLARENCE MANGAN

(1803–1849)

The Nameless One

TELL thou the world, when my bones lie whitening
    Amid the last homes of youth and eld,
That there was once one whose blood ran lightning
      No eye beheld.

And tell how trampled, derided, hated,
And worn by weakness, disease and wrong,
He fled for shelter to God, who mated
      His soul with song.

Go on to tell how, with genius wasted,
Betrayed in friendship, befooled in love,
With spirit shipwrecked and young hopes blasted,
      He still, still strove.

And tell how now, amid wreck and sorrow,
And want and sickness and houseless nights,
He bides in calmness the silent morrow,
      That no ray lights.

And lives he still then? Yes. Old and hoary
At thirty-nine from despair and woe,
He lives enduring what future story
      Will never know.

Him grant a grave to, ye pitying noble,
Deep in your bosoms. There let him dwell.
He too had tears for all souls in trouble
      Here and in Hell.

Dark Rosaleen

O MY Dark Rosaleen!
　　Do not sigh, do not weep!
The priests are on the ocean green,
　　They march along the deep.
There's wine from the royal Pope,
　　Upon the ocean green;
And Spanish ale shall give you hope,
　　My Dark Rosaleen!
　　My own Rosaleen!
Shall glad your heart, shall give you hope,
Shall give you health, and help, and hope,
　　My Dark Rosaleen!

Over hills and through dales
　　Have I roamed for your sake;
All yesterday I sailed with sails
　　On river and on lake.
The Erne, at its highest flood,
　　I dashed across unseen,
For there was lightning in my blood,
　　My Dark Rosaleen!
　　My own Rosaleen!
O there was lightning in my blood,
Red lightning lightened through my blood,
　　My Dark Rosaleen!

All day long in unrest
　　To and fro do I move,
The very heart within my breast
　　Is wasted for you, Love!

JAMES CLARENCE MANGAN

The heart in my bosom faints
    To think of you, my queen !
My life of life, my saint of saints,
    My Dark Rosaleen !
    My own Rosaleen !
To hear your sweet and sad complaints,
My life, my love, my saint of saints,
    My Dark Rosaleen !

Woe and pain, pain and woe,
    Are my lot night and noon;
To see your bright face clouded so,   .
    Like to the mournful moon.
But yet will I rear your throne
    Again in golden sheen:
'Tis you shall reign, shall reign alone,
    My Dark Rosaleen !
    My own Rosaleen !
'Tis you shall have the golden throne,
'Tis you shall reign, and reign alone,
    My Dark Rosaleen !

Over dews, over sands,
    Will I fly for your weal:
Your holy, delicate white hands
    Shall girdle me with steel.
At home, in your emerald bowers,
    From morning's dawn till e'en,
You'll pray for me, my flower of flowers,
    My Dark Rosaleen !
    My fond Rosaleen !

327

You'll think of me through daylight's hours,
My virgin flower, my flower of flowers,
   My Dark Rosaleen !

I could scale the blue air,
   I could plough the high hills,
Oh, I could kneel all night in prayer,
   To heal your many ills.
And one beamy smile from you
   Would float like light between
My toils and me, my own, my true,
   My Dark Rosaleen !
    My fond Rosaleen !
Would give me life and soul anew,
A second life, a soul anew,
   My Dark Rosaleen !

O ! the Erne shall run red
   With redundance of blood,
The earth shall rock beneath our tread,
   And flames wrap hill and wood,
And gun-peal, and slogan-cry,
   Wake many a glen serene,
Ere you shall fade, ere you shall die,
   My Dark Rosaleen !
   My own Rosaleen !
The Judgement Hour must first be nigh,
Ere you can fade, ere you can die,
   My Dark Rosaleen !

JAMES CLARENCE MANGAN

Gone in the Wind

SOLOMON ! where is thy throne ? It is gone in the
   wind.
Babylon ! where is thy might ? It is gone in the wind.
Like the swift shadows of Noon, like the dreams of the Blind,
Vanish the glories and pomps of the earth in the wind.

Man ! canst thou build upon aught in the pride of thy mind ?
Wisdom will teach thee that nothing can tarry behind;
Though there be thousand bright actions embalmed and
   enshrined,
Myriads and millions of brighter are snow in the wind.

Solomon ! where is thy throne ? It is gone in the wind.
Babylon ! where is thy might ? It is gone in the wind.
All that the genius of Man hath achieved and designed
Waits but its hour to be dealt with as dust by the wind.

Pity thou, reader ! the madness of poor Humankind,
Raving of Knowledge,—and Satan so busy to blind !
Raving of Glory,—like me,—for the garlands I bind
(Garlands of song) are but gathered, and—strewn in the wind.

EDWARD WALSH

(1805–1850)

Kitty Bhan

BEFORE the sun rose at yester-dawn
I met a fair maid adown the lawn;
The berry and snow to her cheek gave its glow,
And her bosom was fair as the sailing swan.
Then, pulse of my heart ! what gloom is thine ?

Her beautiful voice more hearts hath won
Than Orpheus' lyre of old hath done:
Her ripe eyes of blue were crystals of dew,
On the grass of the lawn before the sun.
And, pulse of my heart ! what gloom is thine ?

FRANCIS MAHONY, Priest

(1804–1866)

The Bells of Shandon

WITH deep affection and recollection,
  I often think of the Shandon bells,
Whose sounds so wild would, in days of childhood,
  Fling round my cradle their magic spells—
On this I ponder, where'er I wander,
  And thus grow fonder, sweet Cork, of thee;
    With the bells of Shandon,
    That sound so grand on
  The pleasant waters of the river Lee.

I have heard bells chiming full many a clime in,
  Tolling sublime in cathedral shrine;
While at a glib rate brass tongues would vibrate,
  But all their music spoke nought to thine;
For memory dwelling on each proud swelling
  Of thy belfry knelling its bold notes free,
    Made the bells of Shandon
    Sound far more grand on
  The pleasant waters of the river Lee.

I have heard bells tolling " old Adrian's mole " in,
  Their thunder rolling from the Vatican,
With cymbals glorious, swinging uproarious
  In the gorgeous turrets of Notre Dame;
But thy sounds were sweeter than the dome of Peter
  Flings o'er the Tiber, pealing solemnly.
    Oh ! the bells of Shandon
    Sound far more grand on
  The pleasant waters of the river Lee.

FRANCIS MAHONY

There's a bell in Moscow, while on tower and Kiosko,
    In St Sophia the Turkman gets,
And loud in air, calls men to prayer,
    From the tapering summit of tall minarets.
Such empty phantom, I freely grant them,
    But there's an anthem more dear to me,
        It's the bells of Shandon,
            That sound so grand on
        The pleasant waters of the river Lee.

AUBREY DE VERE

(1814–1902)

The Little Black Rose

THE little black rose shall be red at last;
    What made it black but the March wind dry,
And the tear of the widow that fell on it fast?
It shall redden the hills when June is nigh.

The Silk of the Kine shall rest at last;
What drove her forth but the dragon-fly?
In the golden vale she shall feed full fast
With her mild gold horn and slow dark eye.

The wounded wood dove lies dead at last!
The pine long bleeding it shall not die!
This song is secret—mine ear it passed
In a wind on the plains at Athenry.

AUBREY DE VERE

The Sacraments of Nature

FOR we the mighty mountain plains have trod
Both in the glow of sunset and sunrise,
And lighted by the moon of southern skies.
The snow-white torrent of the thundering flood
We two have watched together. In the wood
We two have felt the warm tears dim our eyes,
While zephyrs softer than an infant's sighs
Ruffled the light air of our solitude.
O Earth, maternal Earth, and thou, O Heaven,
And Night, first born, who now, e'en now, dost waken
The host of stars, thy constellated train,
Tell me if these can ever be forgiven,
Those abject, who together have partaken
These Sacraments of Nature—and in vain.

AUBREY DE VERE

A Year of Sorrow

FALL, snow, and cease not! Flake by flake
The decent winding sheet compose;
Thy task is just and pious; make
An end of blasphemies and woes.

Fall, flake by flake! by thee alone
Last friend the sleeping draught is given;
Kind nurse by thee the couch is strewn,
The couch whose covering is from Heaven.

Descend, and clasp the mountain's crest;
Inherit plain and valley deep;
This night on thy maternal breast
A vanquished nation dies in sleep.

Lo! from the starry Temple Gates
Death rides, and bears the flag of peace:
The combatants he separates;
He bids the wrath of ages cease.

     *   *   *

Fall, snow! in stillness fall like dew
On church's roof and cedar's fan;
And mould thyself on pine and yew,
And on the awful face of man.

     *   *   *

On quaking moor and mountain moss,
With eyes upstaring at the sky;
And arms extended like a cross,
The long-expectant sufferers lie.

335

AUBREY DE VERE

Bend o'er them, white-robed acolyte !
Put forth thine hand from cloud and mist;
And minister the last sad Rite,
Where altar there is none, nor priest.

AUBREY DE VERE

The Sun God

I SAW the Master of the Sun. He stood
High in his luminous car, himself more bright,
An Archer of immeasurable might.
On his left shoulder hung his quivered load,
Spurned by his steeds the eastern mountain glowed,
Forward his eager eye and brow of light
He bent; and, while both hands that arch embowed,
Shaft after shaft pursued the flying Night.
No wings profaned that godlike form; around
His neck high held an ever-moving crowd
Of locks hung glistening; while such perfect sound
Fell from his bowstring that th' ethereal dome
Thrilled as a dewdrop; and each passing cloud
Expanded, whitening like the ocean foam.

M

DENIS FLORENCE McCARTHY

(1817–1882)

The Dead Tribune

IN Genoa the superb O'Connell dies,
  That city of Columbus by the sea,
Beneath the canopy of azure skies,
As high and cloudless as his fame must be.
Is it mere chance or higher destiny
That brings these names together ?   One the bold
Wanderer in ways that none had trod but he;
The other, too, exploring paths untold;
One a new world would seek, and one
Would save the old !

DENIS FLORENCE McCARTHY

Spring Flowers from Ireland

WITHIN the letter's rustling fold
   I find once more—a glad surprise—
A little tiny cup of gold,
   Two lovely violet eyes;
A cup of gold with emeralds set,
   Once filled with wine from happier spheres;
Two little eyes so lately wet
   With Spring's delicious dewy tears.

O little eyes that wept and laughed,
   Now bright with smiles, with tears now dim:
O little cup that once was quaffed
   By fay-queens fluttering round thy rim.
I press each silken fringe's fold;
   Sweet little eyes, once more ye shine;
I kiss thy lip, O cup of gold,
   And find thee full of memory's wine.

Within their violet depths I gaze,
   And see, as in the camera's gloom,
The Island with its belt of bays,
   Its chieftained heights all capped with broom;
Which, as the living lens it fills,
   Now seems a giant charmed to sleep,
Now a broad shield embossed with hills
   Upon the bosom of the deep.

DENIS FLORENCE McCARTHY

The vision spreads, the memories grow,
Fair phantoms crowd the more I gaze.
O cup of gold with wine o'erflow !
I'll drink to those departed days;
And when I drain the golden cup
To them, to those, I ne'er can see,
With wine of hope I'll fill it up,
And drink to days that yet may be.

JOHN BOYLE O'REILLY

(1844–1890)

Experience

THE world was made when a man was born,
He must taste for himself the forbidden springs;
He can never take warning from old-fashioned things;
He must fight as a boy, he must drink as a youth,
He must kiss, he must love, he must swear to the truth
Of the friend of his soul; he must laugh to scorn
The hints of deceit in a woman's eyes,
They are clear as the wells of Paradise.

And so he goes on till the world grows old,
Till his tongue has grown cautious, his heart has grown cold,
Till the smile leaves his mouth, till the ring leaves his laugh,
And he shirks the bright headache you ask him to quaff.
He grows formal with men, and with women polite,
And distrustful of both when they're out of his sight.
Then he eats for his palate and drinks for his head,
And loves for his pleasure, and 'tis time he was dead.

JOHN BOYLE O'REILLY

Song

LOVE was true to me,
　　True and tender;
I who ought to be
Love's defender
Let the cold winds blow
Till they chilled him;
Let the winds and snow
Shroud him—and I know
That I killed him.

Years he cried to me
To be kinder;
I was blind to see
And grew blinder.
Years with soft hands raised
Fondly reaching,
Wept and prayed and praised,
Still beseeching.

When he died I woke,
God ! how lonely,
When the grey dawn broke
On one only.
Now beside Love's grave
I am kneeling;
All he sought and gave
I am feeling.

JOHN BOYLE O'REILLY

Disappointment

HER hair was a waving bronze and her eyes
    Deep wells that might cover a brooding soul;
And who, till he weighed it, could ever surmise
That her heart was a cinder instead of a coal?

A White Rose

THE red rose whispers of passion,
    And the white rose breathes of love;
O, the red rose is a falcon,
    And the white rose is a dove.

But I send you a cream-white rosebud,
    With a flush on its petal tips;
For the love that is purest and sweetest
    Has a kiss of desire on the lips.

JOSEPH MARY PLUNKETT

(EXECUTED 1916)

"*Sic Transit*"

THE glories of the world sink down in gloom
And Babylon and Nineveh and all
Of Hell's high strongholds answer to the call,
The silent waving of a sable plume.
But there shall break a day when Death shall loom
For thee, and thine own panoply appal
Thee, like a stallion in a burning stall,
While blood-red stars blaze out in skies of doom.

Lord of sarcophagus and catacomb,
Blood-drunken Death! Within the columned hall
Of time, thou diest when its pillars fall.
Death of all deaths! Thou diggest thine own tomb,
Makest thy mound of Earth's soon-shattered dome,
And pullest the heavens upon thee for a pall.

THOMAS MACDONAGH

(EXECUTED 1916)

Song

LOVE is cruel, Love is sweet,
   Cruel sweet !
Lovers sigh till lovers meet,
   Sigh and meet.
Sigh and meet and sigh again,
Cruel sweet !   O sweetest pain !

Love is blind, but Love is shy,
   Blind and shy;
Thoughts are bold but words are shy,
   Bold and shy.
Bold and shy and bold again,
Sweet is boldness, shyness, pain

M 2

TOM KETTLE

(FELL IN ACTION 1916)

The Lady of Life

I SAT with her, and spoke right goldenly
  Of love and beauty, and because her hair
Brushed me, I plucked down Sirius like a pear,
To braid it, and had laughter for my fee;
Yea, suing her to heavier slavery,
  Had all but plucked the fruitage of her lips,
When lo ! inked clouds and absolute eclipse,
Courteous but unmistakeable ennui.

Then did I mind me of the sorrow wailed
Thro' poets' books, and how the streaming torch
Of suns greater than Sirius has failed,
And as I shambled out the menials' door
I heard new feet sound in the statued porch
And salutations I had heard before.

TOM KETTLE

Parnell's Memory

TEARS will betray all pride, but when ye mourn him
  Be it in soldier wise;
As for a captain who hath gently borne him,
And in the midnight dies.

Fewness of words is best; he was too great
For ours or any phrase.
Love could not guess nor the slipped hound of hate
Track that soul's secret ways.

Signed with a sign, unbroken, unrevealed,
His Calvary he trod.
So let him keep, where all world-wounds are healed,
The silences of God.

He taught us more, this best as it was last:
When comrades go apart
They shall go greatly, cancelling the past,
Slaying the kindlier heart.

Friendship and love, all clean things and unclean,
Shall be as drifted leaves,
Spurned by our Ireland's feet, that queenliest Queen
Who gives not but receives.

FRANCIS LEDWIDGE

(FELL IN ACTION 1917)

The Herons

AS I was climbing Ardan Mor
    From the shore of Sheelan lake,
I met the herons coming down
Before the waters wake.

And they were talking in their flight
Of dreamy ways the herons go
When all the hills are withered up
Nor any waters flow.

THE LITERARY MOVEMENT

WILFRID SCAWEN BLUNT

(1840-1922)

The Falcon

BRAVE as a falcon and as merciless,
  With bright eyes watching still the world, thy prey,
I saw thee pass in thy lone majesty,
Untamed, unmated, high above the press.
The dull crowd gazed at thee. It could not guess
The secret of thy proud aerial way,
Or read in thy mute face the soul which lay
A prisoner there in chains of tenderness.
—Lo, thou art captured. In my hand to-day
I hold thee, and awhile thou deignest to be
Pleased with my jesses. I would fain beguile
My foolish heart to think thou lovest me. See,
I dare not love thee quite. A little while
And thou shalt sail back heavenwards. Woe is me !

WILFRID SCAWEN BLUNT

The Sinner-Saint

IF I have since done evil in my life,
 I was not born for evil. This I know.
My soul was a thing pure from sensual strife.
No vice of the blood foredoomed me to this woe.
I did not love corruption. Beauty, truth,
Justice, compassion, peace with God and man,
These were my laws, the instincts of my youth,
And hold me still, conceal it as I can.
I did not love corruption, nor do love.
I find it ill to hate and ill to grieve.
Nature designed me for a life above
The mere discordant dreams in which I live.
If I now go a beggar on the Earth,
I was a saint of Heaven by right of birth.

WILFRID SCAWEN BLUNT

Gibraltar

SEVEN weeks of sea, and twice seven days of storm
　Upon the huge Atlantic, and once more
We ride into still water and the calm
Of a sweet evening screened by either shore
Of Spain and Barbary. Our toils are o'er,
Our exile is accomplished. Once again
We look on Europe, mistress as of yore
Of the fair Earth and of the hearts of men.
Ay, this is the famed rock, which Hercules
And Goth and Moor bequeathed us. At this door
England stands sentry. God ! to hear the shrill
Sweet treble of her fifes upon the breeze
And at the summons of the rock guns roar
To see her red coats marching from the hill.

OSCAR WILDE

" *Quia Multum Amavi* "

DEAR Heart, I think the young impassioned priest
When first he takes from out the hidden shrine
His God imprisoned in the Eucharist,
And eats the bread, and drinks the dreadful wine,

Feels not such awful wonder as I felt
When first my smitten eyes beat full on thee,
And all night long before thy feet I knelt
Till thou wert wearied of Idolatry.

Ah ! had'st thou liked me less and loved me more,
Through all those summer days of joy and rain,
I had not now been sorrow's heritor,
Or stood a lackey in the House of Pain.

Yet, though remorse, youth's white-faced seneschal,
Tread on my heels with all his retinue,
I am most glad I loved thee—think of all
The suns that go to make one speedwell blue !

OSCAR WILDE

The Ballad of Reading Gaol

(V)

I KNOW not whether Laws be right,
  Or whether Laws be wrong;
All that we know who lie in gaol
Is that the wall is strong;
And that each day is like a year,
A year whose days are long.

But this I know, that every Law
That men have made for Man,
Since first Man took his brother's life,
And the sad world began,
But straws the wheat and saves the chaff
With a most evil fan.

This too I know—and wise it were
If each could know the same—
That every prison that men build
Is built with bricks of shame,
And bound with bars lest Christ should see
How men their brothers maim.

With bars they blur the gracious moon,
And blind the goodly sun:
And they do well to hide their Hell,
For in it things are done
That Son of God nor son of Man
Ever should look upon !

357

OSCAR WILDE

The vilest deeds like poison weeds
Bloom well in prison-air:
It is only what is good in Man
That wastes and withers there:
Pale Anguish keeps the heavy gate,
And the Warder is Despair.

For they starve the little frightened child
Till it weeps both night and day:
And they scourge the weak, and flog the fool,
And gibe the old and gray,
And some grow mad, and all grow bad,
And none a word may say.

Each narrow cell in which we dwell
Is a foul and dark latrine,
And the fetid breath of living Death
Chokes up each grated screen,
And all, but Lust, is turned to dust
In Humanity's machine.

The brackish water that we drink
Creeps with a loathsome slime,
And the bitter bread they weigh in scales
Is full of chalk and lime,
And Sleep will not lie down, but walks
Wild-eyed, and cries to Time.

But though lean Hunger and green Thirst
Like asp with adder fight,
We have little care of prison fare,
For what chills and kills outright
Is that every stone one lifts by day
Becomes one's heart by night.

358

With midnight always in one's heart,
And twilight in one's cell,
We turn the crank, or tear the rope,
Each in his separate Hell,
And the silence is more awful far
Than the sound of a brazen bell.

And never a human voice comes near
To speak a gentle word:
And the eye that watches through the door
Is pitiless and hard:
And by all forgot, we rot and rot,
With soul and body marred.

And thus we rust Life's iron chain
Degraded and alone:
And some men curse, and some men weep,
And some men make no moan:
But God's eternal Laws are kind
And break the heart of stone.

And every human heart that breaks,
In prison-cell or yard,
Is as that broken box that gave
Its treasure to the Lord,
And filled the unclean leper's house
With the scent of costliest nard.

Ah ! happy they whose hearts can break
And peace of pardon win !
How else may man make straight his plan
And cleanse his soul from sin ?
How else but through a broken heart
May Lord Christ enter in ?

And he of the swollen purple throat,
And the stark and staring eyes,
Waits for the holy hands that took
The Thief to Paradise;
And a broken and a contrite heart
The Lord will not despise.

The man in red who reads the Law
Gave him three weeks of life,
Three little weeks in which to heal
The soul of his soul's strife,
And cleanse from every blot of blood
The hand that held the knife.

And with tears of blood he cleansed the hand,
The hand that held the steel:
For only blood can wipe out blood,
And only tears can heal:
And the crimson stain that was of Cain
Became Christ's snow-white seal.

ERNEST DOWSON

(1867–1900)

To One in Bedlam

WITH delicate mad hands behind his sordid bars,
　　Surely he hath his posies, which they tear and twine;
Those scentless wisps of straw, that miserably line
His strait, caged universe, whereat the dull world stares,

Pedant and pitiful.　O, how his rapt gaze wars
With their stupidity!　Know they what dreams divine
Lift his long, laughing reveries like enchanted wine,
And make his melancholy germain to the stars?

O lamentable brother! if those pity thee,
Am I not fain of all thy lone eyes promise me;
Half a fool's kingdom, far from men who sow and reap,
All their days, vanity?　Better than mortal flowers
Thy moon-kissed roses seem: better than love or sleep
The star-crowned solitude of thine oblivious hours!

Epigram

BECAUSE I am idolatrous and have besought,
　　With grievous supplication and consuming prayer,
The admirable image that my dreams have wrought
Out of her swan's neck and her dark abundant hair;
The jealous gods, who brook no worship save their own,
Turned my live idol marble and her heart to stone.

ERNEST DOWSON

Extreme Unction

UPON the eyes, the lips, the feet,
  On all the passages of sense,
The atoning oil is spread with sweet
Renewal of lost innocence.

The feet that lately ran so fast
To meet desire, are soothly sealed;
The eyes that were so often cast
On vanity, are touched and healed.

From troublous sights and sounds set free;
In such a twilight hour of breath,
Shall one retrace his life or see,
Through shadows, the true face of death?

Vials of mercy, sacring oils,
I know not where nor when I come,
Nor through what wanderings and toils,
To crave of you Viaticum.

Yet, when the walls of flesh grow weak,
In such an hour it well may be,
Through mist and darkness, light will break,
And each anointed sense will see.

LIONEL JOHNSON

(1867–1902)

The Dark Angel

*D*ARK *Angel*, with thine aching lust
　　To rid the world of penitence:
Malicious Angel, who still dost
My soul such subtile violence !

Because of thee, no thought, no thing,
Abides for me undesecrate:
Dark Angel, ever on the wing,
Who never reachest me too late !

When music sounds, then changest thou
Its silvery to a sultry fire:
Nor will thine envious heart allow
Delight untortured by desire.

Through thee, the gracious Muses turn
To Furies, O mine Enemy !
And all the things of beauty burn
With flames of evil ecstasy,

Because of thee, the land of dreams
Becomes a gathering place of fears:
Until tormented slumber seems
One vehemence of useless tears.

When sunlight glows upon the flowers,
Or ripples down the dancing sea:
Thou, with thy troop of passionate powers,
Beleaguerest, bewilderest, me.

LIONEL JOHNSON

Within the breath of autumn woods,
Within the winter silences:
Thy venomous spirit stirs and broods,
O Master of impieties !

The ardour of red flame is thine,
And thine the steely soul of ice:
Thou poisonest the fair design
Of nature, with unfair device.

Apples of ashes, golden bright;
Waters of bitterness, how sweet !
O banquet of a foul delight,
Prepared by thee, *dark Paraclete.*

Thou art the whisper in the gloom,
The hinting tone, the haunting laugh:
Thou art the adorner of my tomb,
The minstrel of mine epitaph.

I fight thee, in the Holy Name !
Yet, what thou dost, is what God saith.
Tempter ! should I escape thy flame,
Thou wilt have helped my soul from Death

The second Death, that never dies,
That cannot die, when time is dead:
Live Death, wherein the lost soul cries,
Eternally uncomforted.

LIONEL JOHNSON

Dark Angel, with thine aching lust
Of two defeats, of two despairs:
Less dread, a change to drifting dust,
Than thine eternity of cares.

Do what thou wilt, thou shalt not so,
Dark Angel! triumph over me:
Lonely, unto the Lone I go ;
Divine, to the Divinity.

LIONEL JOHNSON

The Precept of Silence

I KNOW you: solitary griefs,
  Desolate passions, aching hours,
I know you: tremulous beliefs,
Agonized hopes, and ashen flowers!

The winds are sometimes sad to me;
The starry spaces, full of fear:
Mine is the sorrow on the sea,
And mine the sigh of places drear.

Some players upon plaintive strings
Publish their wistfulness abroad:
I have not spoken of these things,
Save to one man, and unto God.

LIONEL JOHNSON

" *Te Martyrum Candidatus* "

AH, see the fair chivalry come, the companions of Christ
  White Horsemen, who ride on white horses, the
Knights of God !
They, for their Lord and their Lover who sacrificed
All, save the sweetness of treading where He first trod !

These through the darkness of death, the dominion of night,
Swept, and they woke in white places at morning tide:
They saw with their eyes, and sang for joy of the sight,
They saw with their eyes the Eyes of the Crucified.

Now, whithersoever He goeth, with Him they go:
White Horsemen, who ride on white horses, oh fair to see !
They ride, where the Rivers of Paradise flash and flow,
White Horsemen, with Christ their Captain: for ever He !

AUBREY BEARDSLEY

(1872–1898)

The Three Musicians

ALONG the path that skirts the wood,
 The three musicians wend their way,
Pleased with their thoughts, each other's mood,
Franz Himmel's latest roundelay,
The morning's work, a new-found theme, their breakfast
  and the summer day.

One's a soprano, lightly frocked
In cool, white muslin that just shows
Her brown silk stockings gaily clocked,
Plump arms and elbows tipped with rose,
And frills of petticoats and things, and outlines as the
  warm wind blows.

Beside her a slim, gracious boy
Hastens to mend her tresses' fall,
And dies her favour to enjoy,
And dies for *réclame* and recall
At Paris and St Petersburg, Vienna and St James' Hall

The third's a Polish pianist
With big engagements everywhere,
A light heart and an iron wrist,
And shocks and shoals of yellow hair,
And fingers that can thrill on sixths and fill beginners
  with despair.

AUBREY BEARDSLEY

The three musicians stroll along
And pluck the ears of ripened corn,
Break into odds and ends of song,
And mock the woods with Siegfried's horn,
And fill the air with Glück, and fill the tweeded tourist's
   soul with scorn.

The Polish genius lags behind,
And, with some poppies in his hand,
Picks out the strings and wood and wind
Of an imaginary band,
Enchanted that for once his men obey his beat and
   understand.

The charming cantatrice reclines
And rests a moment where she sees
Her château's roof that hotly shines
Amid the dusky summer trees,
And fans herself, half shuts her eyes and smooths her
   frock about her knees.

The gracious boy is at her feet,
And weighs his courage with his chance;
His fears soon melt in noonday heat.
The tourist gives a furious glance,
Red as his guide-book grows, moves on, and offers up
   a prayer for France.

FINAL DIRGE

THIS ae night, this ae night,
    Every night and all,
Fire and sleet and candle-light,
And Christ receive thy saule.

When thou from hence away art past,
    Every night and all,
To Whinny-muir thou com'st at last;
And Christ receive thy saule.

If ever thou gavest hosen and shoon,
    Every night and all,
Sit thee down and put them on;
And Christ receive thy saule.

If hosen and shoon thou ne'er gav'st nane,
    Every night and all,
The whins shall prick thee to the bare bane;
And Christ receive thy saule.

From Whinny-muir when thou may'st pass,
    Every night and all,
To Brig o' Dread thou com'st at last,
And Christ receive thy saule.

From Brig o' Dread when thou may'st pass,
    Every night and all,
To Purgatory fire thou com'st at last,
And Christ receive thy saule.

FINAL DIRGE

If ever thou gavest meat or drink,
Every night and all,
The fire shall never make thee shrink;
And Christ receive thy saule.

If meat and drink thou ne'er gav'st nane,
Every night and all,
The fire will burn thee to the bare bane,
And Christ receive thy saule.

This ae night, this ae night,
Every night and all,
Fire and sleet and candle-light,
And Christ receive thy saule.